TRUE LIFE WONDER

TRUE LIFE WONDER

A true story of surviving the most
difficult yet rewarding times on earth.
The Biography of Suzanne Smith

A BIOGRAPHY

By
Suzanne Smith

MILL CITY PRESS

Mill City Press, Inc.
2301 Lucien Way #415
Maitland, FL 32751
407.339.4217
www.millcitypress.net

Printed in the United States of America

ISBN-13: 978-1-54564-863-6

In memory of my mother,
Mom
For my children,
Daniel and Cathy and
Grandchildren,
Ericka Tanya Aaron,
Samantha Joshua and Jacob

TABLE OF CONTENTS

PREFACE

I n this biography I present my endless mem-
ories of my native country, Vietnam, and the true
wonders in the life of my mother and myself beginning
in Vietnam in 1905 and continuing to the present day
in the United States of America. Many excellent books
have been written on Vietnam, most of them focusing
on specific stories of the American involvement in the
1960's/1970's war there or of different spans of time
in the country's history. I write from a very different
perspective in that my words and actions describe the
very personal lives of two persons and their families
who survived the most difficult yet rewarding times
of their life on earth. For understanding of the many
influences affecting our lives I intentionally begin with
a general description of our country, the development
of the language, the unusual diversity in religions and
the related industries and exports. I follow with the life
of my mother, a remarkable lady, who suffered from
early childhood through many years of family abuse,
hard work and ethereal happenings. My life began with
a truly heavenly virgin birth, described by my mother.
which I continue to question. I follow with my early

years of maturing with very definite guidance from God, taking advantage of limited personal opportunities and routinely a step ahead of my peers. My early knowledge of the English language provided many opportunities to work with Americans arriving in Vietnam in support of the war. Through demonstrated job performance I was able to rapidly advance to positions of more responsibility and increased attention to my professional abilities. During this time I met the father of my children who subsequently left me to raise our twin boy and girl alone. At the end of the war in Vietnam a TV journalist recorded my plight with my children. This show received wide publicity in the United States. The very popular attention given that brief show was the impetus that allowed me a miraculous escape from Vietnam, with my children, and to eventually settle in the United States. Over the following years I have continued my formal education and expanded my professional skills. I have rapidly assumed increased positions of responsibility. My children have taken advantage of the new world around them. They now have their own families and I have settled into a comfortable, enjoyable, and productive life style. I continue to do God's work.

VIETNAM

My mother and I were born in Vietnam, one of the most beautiful countries in South East Asia, with a country side like a page out of the Bible and the people equally exotic. To better understand our involvement in this arena I first provide a review of the history and the involved factions that contributed to our lives.

THE GEOGRAPHY

For 80 years under the French colonial system Vietnam was divided into the Protectorate of Tonkin in the North, the northern mountain area, the Protectorate of Annam in the Center, the central highlands, and Cochin China in the South, the southern delta region. For many past years this area was referred to as French Indochina. The country of Vietnam is shaped like an

2

elongated letter S, bounded on the East by the Gulf of Tonkin and the South China Sea. The western boundary of Vietnam borders the countries of Cambodia in the South, Laos in the mid-section and China on the North, covering an area of over 128,000 square miles.

The Northern area is known for the Alpine like peaks, waterfalls, caves and rich mineral deposits. The Red River flows from China through deep gorges and thick forests to the Gulf of Tonkin. Astride the Red River is the city of Hanoi where the exotic chic of old Asia blends with the dynamic face of new Asia. In Hanoi the medieval and modern co-exist with a blend of Asian peace and Parisian grace. The city is an architectural museum piece evolving in harmony with its history. The Red River Delta is where the rice rich plains of Cao Bang and Vinh Yen and the busy sea port of Hai Phong meet the Gulf of Tonkin. Just north along the sea coast, is Ha Long Bay, where thousands of limestone pinnacles in strange geological formations protrude from the sea.

Central Vietnam is characterized by high, temperate plateaus, rich in volcanic soil and by beautiful beaches, dunes and lagoons. On the coast lies the ancient Imperial City of Hue which was the heartland of the ancient Kingdom of Champa. Here you will find ruins of the old temples, royal tombs, pagodas and the Cathedral of Hue. Hue for centuries was the center of Imperial Reign over the people of Vietnam. This was the home of Bao Dai, the last Emperor of Vietnam. He was an ineffectual ruler who collaborated with the Japanese during World War II, worked with the Viet Minh and cooperated with the French to accomplish their aims. Just north of Hue, at the 17th parallel, on 22 July, 1954, the Demilitarized Zone was established separating North and South Vietnam. South of Hue is the city of Danang which was a major seaport for the early Portuguese and Spanish traders and theologians. Today Danang, with an international airport, is a popular entry for tourists visiting the sites of the bloody battles of the Vietnam War.

Further South in the Central Highlands, West of the port of Cam Ranh Bay, is the city of Dalat at an elevation of 1,475 meters with a population of some 200,000. The area remains populated by different sects of mountain people called Montagnards. Dalat is surrounded by beautiful mountain vistas, waterfalls, evergreen forests and gardens. Local products include silk, garden vegetables and flowers. This is a great part of the country to see on the back of a motorbike, stopping at will to view the countryside. During the Vietnam War Dalat was the home of the training center for the officers of the South Vietnamese Army.

The Southern Delta Region stretches from just North of Ho Chi Minh City, formerly known as Saigon, to the south tip of the Camau Peninsula. The region is bisected by the Mekong River. This river rises in the Tibetan plateau and flows over 2,700 miles encompassing six countries of Southeast Asia. The river initially, in China in the North, traverses through Myanmar then forms the Vietnamese border between Laos and Thailand, then flows through Cambodia and enters Vietnam. It forms the largest river delta in the world, the Mekong Delta, before emptying into the South China Sea. The Vietnamese call it Song Cuu Long which translated means River of Nine Dragons. The rice paddies of the delta area are some of the richest in the world. Apart from rice, the Mekong Delta is also used for commercial fishing. A giant catfish is the most popular, known as "Mekong Catfish", which could grow up to 10 feet long. Also found in the river delta are many species of turtles, water snakes and insects. The Mekong Delta is a rich area for raising animals such as pigs, ducks, chickens and some cattle.

Ho Chi Minh City is Vietnam's largest metropolis and the undisputed center of commerce and trade. The city is booming with international industries, lavish hotels and fancy restaurants. Thousands of motorbikes fly along the streets teeming with sidewalk markets. Two hours by motorbike south of Ho Chi Minh City, along the northern tributary of the Mekong River, is the city of My Tho. Here you will see a central market and many floating markets selling the varied fruits and vegetables of the area. My Tho is the capital of Tien Giang Province where you will find the temple of the Cao Dai religious sect. Further south, along the southern tributary of the Mekong River is the city of Can Tho, the largest city along the Mekong. Here are larger streets and waterfront markets selling everything from cigarettes to fruits and vegetables. Can Tho is now a very popular town for tourists with ferry boat trips on the river.

During the early 1940's, the impact of World War II affected the lives of all Vietnamese. The Japanese Empire took over the French administration of French Indochina imprisoning, killing and torturing many Frenchmen and Vietnamese who worked for the French. The Japanese placed Emperor Bao Dai in control and he served them as a puppet leader, the same as he had served the French. Following the Japanese surrender to the Allies in 1945, soon after the United States used Atomic Bombs on Hiroshima and Nagasaki, Japan, many

Vietnamese responded to the call of Ho Chi Minh for resistance to a French re-invasion. That group, led by the Communist, appealed to the nationalist sentiments of the Vietnamese people. That group was called The Vietnamese Independence League later known as the Viet Minh. In the Mekong Delta area most of the peasants who had supported the Viet Minh against the French were Nationalist not Communist. The primary interest of the villager was to tend his crops and to take care of his family.

In 1954 the country of Vietnam was divided into two zones. The southern area, called the Republic of Vietnam was led by President Ngo Dinh Diem. His leadership strongly supported the Catholic faith and the Viet Minh saw this as another intrusion upon Vietnamese Nationalism. The Viet Minh convinced many villagers not to support the Government. These villagers began to fight against all elements of the Republic and were labeled "Vietcong". The hit and run tactics of the Vietcong left many dead and villages in ruin. This continued until 1975 when the North defeated the South and reunited the two Vietnams today as a country under Communist domination.

THE LANGUAGE OF VIETNAM

The Vietnamese language (Kinh) is a fusion of different elements of the Mon-Khmer, Thai and Chinese languages. A significant percentage of the basic words come from the Mon-Khmer. From the Thai came certain grammatical elements and tonality. The Chinese provided literary and technical vocabulary as well as a traditional writing system. For centuries the Vietnamese language was written in standard Chinese characters called Chu Nho. Around the 13th century the Vietnamese devised their own writing system created by combining two Chinese words or a single Chinese word using single Chinese characters for their phonic value. Both writing systems were used until the 20th century. During the 17th century, a brilliant French Jesuit scholar, Alexandre de Rhodes, devised a Latin-based phonetic alphabet. De Rhodes was later sentenced to death for entering Vietnam illegally and for his missionary activities. He was expelled from the country but the two priests working with him were beheaded.

In 1905, lead by Phan Boi Chau, a French trained scholar, Vietnam was exposed to Western philosophy. It was his desire to establish an independent republic based on the modern skills of the Vietnamese, Japanese and Chinese. His plan was to send Vietnamese students to Japan to learn modern skills. He wished to counter the pressures of the French. His plan was adopted. Early in the 20th century, Phan Chu Trinh changed the Nom script to the Roman (Quoc Ngu) alphabet. From that time on the present Vietnamese alphabet has been commonly used.

THE RELIGIONS OF VIETNAM

Religion has exerted a strong influence on Vietnamese culture and concept of life. The attitude towards life, death and the world beyond reflects a deep imprint of Buddhism, Confucianism and Taoism. The predominant religion in Vietnam is Buddhism which was introduced into Vietnam under the Chinese domination, in the second century B.C., by Chinese immigrants and by Indian preachers coming by sea. The practice of Buddhism in Vietnam differs from other Asian countries, and does not contain the same institutional structures or hierarchy that exists in other traditional Buddhist settings. It has instead grown from symbiotic relationship with Taoism, Chinese spirituality, and indigenous Vietnamese religion, with the majority of Buddhist practitioners focusing on devotional rituals rather than meditation. The great majority of Vietnamese people regard themselves as Buddhists but not all of them actively participate in Buddhist rituals at the Pagoda. Under the French administration, the Catholics enjoyed the support of the government. It was during the Ngo Dinh Diem regime that the Catholics filled key positions in the government, the army and the police.

Confucianism is more of a religious and social philosophy than a religion in the accepted meaning of the word. It has no church, no clergy and no bible. In the early days the rules of the Confucian leader had to be followed to the letter or the violator and his family would be punished by death. Confucianism advocates a code of social behavior that man ought to observe so as to live in harmony with society and attain happiness in his individual life. There is little concern about death, the world beyond and spiritual feeling in this philosophy. There is an often told story of a woman who remained pregnant for eighty years. She had been impregnated by an angel who combined the elements of the earth, metal, wood, water combined with fire. When the male child was borne its hair was white. This was the beginning of mankind.

Taoism has a deep imprint on the way of life of the Vietnamese. This religion advocates a philosophy of harmony between man and man and between man and nature. To achieve this harmony, all fronts of confrontation must be avoided. The virtues of simplicity, patience and self-contentment must be observed. By non-action and keeping away from human strife and cravings, man can reach harmony with himself, other people and the universe. Taoist clergymen claimed they could cure illness, alleviate misfortune and predict the future. The mystic aspect of Taoism appeals to the common people of Vietnam.

Significant is a religious tradition, Hoa Hao, based on Buddhism, founded in 1939 by Huynh Pho So, a native of the Mekong Delta region of southern Vietnam. Hoa Hao followers were considered to be living Buddas, destined to save mankind from suffering and to protect the Vietnamese nation. Hoa Hao stresses the practice of Buddhism by lay people in the home, rather than focusing on temple worship and ordination. Aid to the poor is favored over fancy pagoda buildings or expensive rituals.

Another religious sect recently established in Vietnam is the Cao Dai. Like the Hoa Hao, the Cao Dai have been confined to the rural sectors of the southern delta region. Caodaism is a synthesis of different beliefs, including the teachings of Buddha, Jesus, Confucius, Lao-Tse, Victor Hugo and others. It was founded in 1919 by Le Van Trung who established a priestly hierarchy modeled along Roman Catholic lines. Adherents engage in ethical practices such as prayer, veneration of ancestors, nonviolence and vegetarianism with the minimum goal of rejoining God the Father in Heaven and the ultimate goal of freedom from the cycle of birth and death. The seat of Caodaism is in Tay Ninh about 60 miles from Ho Chi Minh City. The Cao Dai identify their belief with color. The Buddhists wear yellow, the Tao wear gray, the Confucians wear red and the Christians wear white.

A religion, now defunct in Vietnam, was called the Trinh Do Cu Si. This was a mixture of Christianity and Buddhism. It was started by an interesting personality from the southern delta area of Vietnam, Dao Dua, known as the Coconut Monk. He was given that name as for years his only nourishment was from the coconut tree. Born in the southern province of Kien Hoa in 1909, he received his early education from the French priests in the area. He later studied chemistry and physics in France. On return to Vietnam he married and had a daughter. In 1945 he left his family to pursue a monastic life. For three years he sat on a stone slab on a high pole to meditate. Due to his unusual behavior and influence of those around him, thought to be disruptive, he was imprisoned several times by the Communist government. His last days were spent in his home, a houseboat on the north island of Kien Hoa Province. He died in 1990.

Currently, the Constitution of the Socialist Republic of Vietnam formally allows religious freedom however, the government restrictions remain on organized activities of many religious groups. The government maintains a prominent role overseeing officially recognized religions. Six religions now recognized by the state are: Buddhism, Catholicism, Protestantism, Islam, Cao Dai and Hoa Hao.

INDUSTRIES AND EXPORTS

Rice production in Vietnam in the Mekong and Red River deltas is important to the food supply for the country and the national economy. Rice is a staple of the national diet and is seen as a "gift from God". By the end of World War II, the French had made French Indochina the world's largest rice exporter after Burma and Thailand. Vietnam is now the second largest, exporter worldwide, after Thailand, and the seventh largest consumer of rice. The most prominent irrigated rice system is the Mekong Delta. A total of twelve provinces constitute this area, popularly known as the "Rice Bowl" of Vietnam. Vietnam now exports 4 to 5 million tons of rice a year, throughout the world. Modern mechanized farming methods and new strains of rice are becoming popular. There are more than 1600 varieties of rice grown in the Mekong Delta. One unique variety is the "floating" rice, with several foot long stems which float, keeping it above the rising flood waters of the Mekong Delta. As rice farming becomes more mechanized, traditional wooden farm tools as well as older strains of rice are preserved. Old rice varieties still have a strong characteristic. They can grow in acid sulfate and saline soil and submerged areas. They are tasty and have a popular flavor.

Cooked rice is the main dish for most Vietnamese meals. It is routinely eaten in a dish of meat, fish or vegetables. Rice is the product used to make several types of noodles, rice paper and in the production of wine. Production of a fish sauce (Nuoc Mam) for domestic use and export is a popular commodity. Over 17 million liters a year are produced, with the most desired from the island of Phu Quoc located off the southwest coast.

For many years the production of rubber was the principle export from Vietnam. Rubber is now the second largest export after rice. The Rubber Plantations were owned and operated by the French in the nineteen hundreds. France was the colonial power in Vietnam for many years and the Rubber Plantations were a result of that colonialism. Between 1898 and 1899 the first Rubber Plantations were started near Saigon. It took eight years of engineering and cultivation by the French before production was started. By 1911 there were some 5,000 hectares in plantations and more to be established later.

Plantation Dang, in the Bo Mia area, some 50 miles North West of Saigon, started production in 1928. The very rich soil in that area was a tremendous asset to production. In 1948 the Michelin Rubber Company used the natural rubber in the production of automobile tires. When the French withdrew from Vietnam, leaving the plantations behind, senior Vietnamese in the area, or the plantation managers, took over the activities and reaped large financial profits while the legal ownership was being determined. From the time of the Communist takeover in 1975 until the present day Vietnam has benefited from the assistance of Russia, increasing the acreage and annual production of natural rubber from 55,000 to 95,000 metric tons.

For centuries the artistic talents of the Vietnamese people were expressed in their production of detailed lacquer works, fancy embroideries and sculptors from the sea. The French influenced the use of local materials to create their products and provided a European market for their creations. Today lacquered murals of Asian scenes on very special wooden backing are collector items. Their fancy floral embroidery, hand woven in native silks, linens and like materials, are beautifully displayed in clothing, table coverings, matting and the like. Special collected sea shells are artistically displayed in fancy jewelry products.

Other Vietnamese exports include several tons each year of many species of fish, shrimps, lobsters, oysters, clams and squid. In the central highlands and northern mountains of Vietnam you find mining of precious ores of gold, platinum, silver and mercury. Also precious stones such as emeralds and birthstones are found. Primarily in the North is the mining and production of iron, chrome, copper, zinc, lead and coal. In recent years, in the South, clothing manufacturing has begun to compete in the worldwide market with China and Japan.

EDUCATION

During the early 1800's there was little or no organized education system for the Vietnamese people outside of the teachings of the religious sects. The French, who were in control, were concerned that an educated people would be more difficult to manage and were hesitant to establish an education system for the Vietnamese. In 1871 the French decided to set up a strictly controlled education system for the country of Vietnam and began to train Vietnamese teachers to run their schools as they directed. Whoever was selected to attend these schools was required to strictly obey French rules. They must speak in the French language and use Chinese script. On graduation these Vietnamese teachers would be assigned by the French to specific areas of the country to start their schools. One teacher might be assigned to be responsible for over 20 elementary schools. These teachers were given special treatment and paid well to retain their loyalty.

During this time the French did not allow elementary schools in the smallest villages. Only 6 Provinces had these elementary schools. They were Saigon, Cho Lon, My Tho, Vinh Long, Kien Hoa and Soc Trang. These very few schools were able to educate less than one percent of the population of millions. As the years passed into the mid-1900s, middle schools and high schools were established in the large cities such as Hanoi and Saigon. From 1923 to 1930 the student population rose from 56,000 to 430,000, but this amounted to only 1.8 percent of the country's population of over twenty million.

In the early years many of the Vietnamese could not read or write as this is the way the French wanted it to be. Fortunately there is an inherent psyche of the Vietnamese people to learn. They routinely display a high degree of personal intelligence. They taught themselves, quickly learning from their daily experiences and dealing with the challenges of life. They took advantage of their contact with those having a formal education to expand their knowledge. In many cases they outshone their well educated foreign associates.

In 1916 the French needed Doctors, Nurses and other technicians to support their war effort. The French sent 400 specially selected Vietnamese for training. From this the French learned that they needed a higher level education system in Vietnam. In 1917 the French opened a limited number of Intermediate and High Schools in Vietnam. There were fifteen provinces with four schools, two schools in Hue for girls and another school for girls in Qui Nhon. There were two schools in each of the cities of Hanoi and Saigon. As the years passed, schools for advanced studies in business administration, law, agriculture and general subjects developed. The college level courses were government sponsored and some privately supported. In most cases these schools were so costly that very few could afford to attend. By 1945 the literacy rate of the Vietnamese population had greatly improved. This was greatly attributed to teaching by the French trained Vietnamese teachers. After their day in the French controlled schools these Vietnamese teachers would teach at night those children and adults who desired to learn, in some cases only if it was just to learn to read and write.

From 1945 to 1956 the South Vietnamese government organized an educational system establishing all levels of education from nursery school to university level with graduate, master and doctorate programs. Following the Communist takeover of the country in 1975 the educational system has continued to improve and has contributed to positive development of Vietnam by Vietnamese.

TET NGUYEN DAN (VIETNAMESE LUNAR NEW YEAR)

Most Vietnamese do not celebrate birthdays and Christmas, as we do in the United States, saving the season of Tet for celebration. Tet is the beginning of the Lunar New Year. The lunar month has 29 or 30 days resulting in a 355 day year. The Vietnamese Lunar Calendar closely resembles that of the Chinese. The Vietnamese Lunar Calendar has 12 animals of the Zodiac each representing one year in a twelve year cycle. Every third year, leap year, an extra month is added between the third and fourth month. There is a chart to show in what year a person is born and what Zodiac sign represents that year. The Vietnamese New Year, Tet, annually falls between late January and mid-February. If your date of birth is in the first half of January your Zodiac sign will be that of the previous year.

During Tet, Vietnamese families welcome ancestral spirits and dead relatives home with special yellow, white or pink Cherry blossoms. They place other flowers, foods and fruits on a family alter with burning incense. The food is changed every day. The worshiping continues for three to seven days, from opening day until closing. Tet is a festival of fun. It is a time to visit the cemeteries and the tombs of their relatives. They visit family and friends to get together to review the past and express good wishes for the coming year. A typical token of good luck is passed with some paper money or even just one coin distributed in a small red packet.

In days before Tet there is a special cake prepared. It is called Banh Tet in the South and Ban Chung in the North. This cake is made with fresh sweet rice soaked for at least ten hours. This rice is then wrapped in banana leaves filled with mung beans, pork, onions, ground pepper and salt to taste. The shape of Banh Tet is round and is twenty inches long or longer. The shape of Banh Chung is square. These cakes are sold in the markets everywhere. In addition to Banh Tet you will also find Mut, a sweet dried candy made from pumpkin, coconut, ginger, sweet potato, carrot, pineapple, lotus seed and other vegetables.

Very similar to Tet is the celebration of Mid-Autumn Day. On the fifteenth of the lunar month, a night of the full moon in September, there is display of many types of lanterns and a fun time for the children. There are parades, singing and dancing on the streets and in the schools, village meeting halls and open yards. There is a special cake called "Banh Trung Thu", made with many types of nuts from the Watermelon, Almond, Lotus, Macadamia and others. It also includes dried sweet Pumpkin and whole round egg yolks. Banh Trung Thu, Mung Bean cake and candy are prepared for gifts to family and friends.

On September's full moon day, the Vietnamese people, especially those Buddha and Ancestor worshipers, celebrate the souls of those who have died. They will place incense, fruit and other food stuff outside and pray for luck. After an hour or so they will burn paper clothes and money believing that those dead will wear these clothes and spend that money. Later the fruit and foodstuff will be fed to the children for good luck.

TUNG THI NGO

My mother, Tung Thi Ngo, whom hereafter I call Mom, is the source of endless episodes of her life and mine which I must share with everyone. Some of my descriptions are ethereal but most are very easy to realize and understand. Mom survived over centuries of incursions by the Chinese, French and Japanese and more recently the Viet Minh, Viet Cong and the North Vietnamese Communists. Intertwined with the major aggressions were incessant internal fighting among local religious sects of the Buddhists, Hoa Hao, Cao Dai and Catholics.

Mom was born in 1905 in Can Tho, An Binh Province, along the Mekong River in the Southern Delta area of Vietnam. An orphan, as a baby, she was left at the door of the Ngo family, my grandparents. My grandmother and grandfather were not happy to have this orphaned baby added to their family. At that time the Ngo's already had six children and Mom was designated as number eight child. (In Vietnam the first child is always designated as number two.) As she grew up Mom was continually mistreated by her stepmother, Mui. Mui would frequently falsely accuse Mom of misbehaving in order to have the stepfather, Thin, severely punish her. Many times she went to bed at night black and blue with bruises from beatings. This happened several times a month to the extreme that Mom was frequently so sore that she could not walk. Thin would always believe his wife's accusations and not listen to Mom to hear the true story of what had taken place. The only person to love my Mom was her grandmother. The grandmother was often hit herself when trying to take the whip from Thin beating Mom.

The Ngo's treated Mom worse than a servant. She was required to do most of the house work, care for the garden and take care of the animals. At the age of 14, Mom had to work in the one hundred plus acre Ngo family rice paddy, planting and harvesting rice. She was required to tend the rice barn, while the other children and other workers remained in the house or away. Stepfather, Thin, was over 50 years old. He owned several hundred acres of land and hired many workers to work the rice paddies and fruit orchards. Frequently he would treat them to lunch. Mom had to work hard preparing their food and serving them while they sat around on their soft bamboo mats.

One of the brothers in the family was trained in a very different form of Martial Arts. He could jump very fast and very high from a sitting position. He could leap high to pick fruit from the trees. Responding to one worker's request he leaped high for fruit and delivered a green banana on the worker's plate. He mastered this as a deterrent to a number of robberies they were experiencing in their neighborhood. He was known to be able to catch the thieves and tie their long pony tail like hair to a pole and give them their just rewards.

Thin regularly either roasted or salted down a pork leg. He would always give them to the workers, especially at the time of celebrating Tet. He was very generous giving the workers anything they requested but he never gave anything to Mom. In his early days, Thin was a very rich farmer but as he grew older, due to the use of drugs and gambling, his land, his houses and his money were lost.

As a teenager, Mom was raped by her older brother. She was hurt and bled but dared not yell as she was afraid her mother would hear and punish her. Mom kept quiet and said nothing about the rape to anyone else. Thin did not believe that his daughters needed to go to school. Having a yearning for education, Mom talked Thin into letting her go to the home of an uncle who was a teacher. Unfortunately there she again became a maid and was required to do all kinds of housework. While there she did learn that she had to have a birth certificate to enroll in school. As an orphan, her adop-tive parents had not prepared a birth certificate for her so she could not enroll in school. Her true name was Ngoc Uyen before being called Tung Thi Ngo. She remained at the uncle's home for a few weeks before school was to start. When school started, Thin made her come home as he needed her to work at his house.

Once in a while Mom would stand on the bridge at the school entrance and wait for the children to come out for recess and ask to hold their school bags for just a few minutes. This provided her very brief per-sonal pleasure being close to the books. Mom helped neighbors whenever they had parties and learned much from helping with the cooking and party deco-rations. Mom did not receive any formal education in the local schools but she was very quick to learn from those around her. She was smarter than all the other children in the family. She always had great ideas on how manage things and how to make and save money in her "piggybank". Her bank was a long, large bamboo stick, sealed at both ends with a slot to insert coins. On one occasion when the piggy bank should have been almost full, Mom went to take the money out to buy a few things. To her discuss she found the coins had been stolen by her older brother.

Mom was not only the leader among her brothers and sisters but also lead the neighborhood children and friends. She taught them how to cook, sew and make cloth from dried banana leaves or whatever paper she could find. On occasion, Thin would make Mom go to the store at nighttime to buy oil for the night lights. He did not want his other children to go through the dark jungle but did not care for Mom's feelings. Most persons would not go through the jungle at night for it was very dark and scary. They would see eerie shadows and hear strange noises. Mom had no choice but to go so she would gather neighbors and friends to go with her. Often as they reached the darker and scarier areas of the woods, the noises and shadows would appear. Her friends would panic, cry, and fall as they ran to get out of the woods. Mom always braved the jungle noises. She liked to tell the story about her friends' actions.

Mom was a very pretty young lady and many of the men wanted to date her and even marry her at the age of 18. The step-parents rejected them as they wanted her to marry into a rich family. Also they wanted her to continue in the household to do the chores as in the past. When Mom was 24 years old there was a man who came from a rich family whom her stepparents wanted her to marry. Mom rejected him as he was the son of a Cambodian tribesman. This man became so angry at being rejected that he hired a person to poison Mom.

On one occasion, while Mom was helping her Auntie to sell drinks in her shop, she was asked by a customer to smell the fragrance from a charm bottle. This she refused. The charm bottle was set on her working counter with the top opened. As it started to bubble the hired assassin of the rejected suitor ran away. Mom breathed in the fumes which unknown to her were poisonous. Later, with her evening meal, her food included a serving of bean sprouts. Suddenly blood started coming from her mouth, nose and eyes. Mom almost died. On consulting a "charm" doctor familiar with this type bleeding, he advised that if Mom had not eaten the bean sprouts with her meal she probably would have died. One result, attributed to the poison, was that Mom began to lose her teeth and by the age of 40 she had only 3 teeth left in her mouth.

Tung Thi Ngo, Mom

After years of family abuse Mom was married in 1931 at the age of 26. Her husband, Lam Thien Hoi, was primarily a teacher but a man of many trades and spoke 7 languages fluently. Although limited in his formal education, due to his exceptional personal intellect and ability to learn the many necessities of life, he became a highly respected teacher. Hoi was a handsome playboy, very popular with all the ladies. Very early in their marriage he frequently left Mom, for several months at a time, to be with his other female friends. Mom would usually stay with his parents while he was away. While living with Hoi's parents she was routinely mistreated. They took back most of the jewelry they had given to her at her wedding. They also took most of her nicest clothes.

Hoi and Mom's first child, a son, was born in 1934. At this time he moved Mom out of his parent's home to their own house. He remained with her for a few months but departed again leaving her with no funds. Hoi remained away this time until the son was almost two years old. Mom had to catch fish and shrimp to have food for her child and herself. She would buy fruit cheap and resell for a little profit. She had a good neighbor who watched her son while she was away from home. When Hoi came home again he remained until their second child was born. Hoi soon left again with Mom pregnant and did not return until their third child was two years old. On this occasion he remained home for about 4 months. He did not work or help Mom selling food.

Hoi spent most of this time hiding from a Frenchman because he was fooling around with the Frenchman's girl friend. The Frenchman found Hoi and was going to attack him but Hoi was able to escape by jumping from a third floor window. Hoi was injured in the fall and returned home so Mom could take care of his injury. After healing he worked for a German for a while and again left home with Mom pregnant with their fourth child. Hoi disappeared for several years. It was very hard for Mom to take care of four children by herself. She became so upset that when any of the children disturbed her she would get very angry. On one occasion she threw a knife at my third sister and then threw her in the lake. Fortunately a passerby saved my little sister otherwise she would have drowned.

When their first child was nine years old, as a young boy, he went to school and also worked to help Mom. He would catch wild birds and gather bird eggs, crickets and grasshoppers to sell. He helped to raise pigs which were kept in the house. The pigs were very smart and were trained to watch the house. The pigs would obey the commands of Mom and my brother.

During this time the Vietcong were sneaking into their town at night and murdering those who showed support for the government. Due to the hit and run fighting tactics of the Vietcong, on one occasion the family had to desert their home for a few weeks. When they returned the house had been ransacked, and had almost collapsed. Mom had to gather bamboo poles and palm fronds to rebuild her house. Almost everything in the house was gone. The clothes of Mom and the children had been ripped apart and they were left with nothing to wear. Mom gathered patches of cloth and was able to get some cloth from neighbors to make clothing for the children and her clothes. The fourth child was almost two years old and Mom had no word from Hoi. She did not know where he was. Hoi was gone again for over two years and Mom continued to work very hard, long hours each day, to house and feed her children.

In early 1945 Mom sat on a thick wooden bed overlooking a canal, feeling very sad and worried. Suddenly, a very bright, fairy like image (Ba Set) flew in front of her. She saw a brilliant blue, yellow and red shining light which came directly to her and then instantly disappeared. She knew that it was not a ghost or someone trying to scare her. Mom's whole body trembled with unusual feelings and she could not figure what it was all about. Mom went to her third sister's home and described the incident to her. The sister told Mom that this was a bad sign for her and that soon bad luck and something terrible would happen to her.

After a while Mom's stomach started growing as if she was pregnant. She first thought she was just getting fat but soon her whole body was trembling and she knew that she was pregnant. She did not get morning sickness like in her other pregnancies. Mom could not understand why she was pregnant since she had not had sexual intercourse since the birth of her fourth child. Mom felt very sad and cried and began to wonder and think that God (Ong Troi), had been involved. She prayed to God. This encouraged her to live.

Mom said nothing to anyone about this, pretending it was a normal pregnancy as she was a married woman. In September, 1945, at about 3:30 AM, Mom gave birth to me. She had to wait several hours for a midwife to arrive. My brother and a neighbor had to go by boat, two hours each way, to get the midwife. She was a very popular, experienced and professional midwife who was over 70 years old. On arrival she immediately cut the umbilical cord and took the necessary care for Mom and me.

As ethereal as it appeared to be, my entry into this world, as described in much detail to me by Mom, was an Immaculate Conception, a virgin birth. This entire event was described to me in detailed visions from God. My Mom had kept this event a secret from everyone. When I asked her about the vision I had received she admitted the events were true as had been described to me. Although born in September, 1945, I did not have a birth certificate until December, 1947.

The war became more violent and Mom and children had to evacuate our home again. At this time not only was there fighting between the Viet Minh and the government but also struggles between the religious sects of the Hoa Hao and the Cao Dai. On one occasion, when we went to the fields to hide, Mom took all the doors of our house down so the Hoa Hao could not hide from their enemies. On return our house was empty again. The Hoa Hao had stolen everything, even chopped down our fruit trees for fire wood. The neighbor's house was done the same.

Mom and her son knew when and how to catch edible fish and shrimp while in their canoe. Many times they would fill their canoe with their catch but Mom knew when to stop. Others were so greedy, even though Mom had warned them not to take too much, they would take on so many fish that their canoe would tip over and sink. They frequently had many buckets of fish from the canals, the creek and the main river.

Mom usually went fishing with the other family teams. On one occasion she went alone to the river and was almost killed by the Hoa Hao. While she was in the river fishing at low tide, the Hoa Hao fighters, assuming she was supporting their enemies, tied her to a post in the river to watch her drown when the tide came in. Mom told them that if they proceeded to drown her they must also drown her four children as they would die without her care. Hearing her plea they let her go. Later, several times they would bring a human head to her home for her to recognize and to admit that it was her relative. She would always say no even though she knew they were from her family. This saved her children and herself from being murdered.

Time went by and Mom continued working very hard to feed her children. Mom's second daughter took care of me while Mom was working. When I was hungry and cried, she would put thick cooked rice juice mixed with sugar in a bottle to feed me. When Mom came home from work late at night she would breast feed me. As I grew up Mom would often tell me about the fairy like images coming from the sky with shining lights. She would point out the beautiful palms by the canal where the fairy like images, she now described as angels, appeared. Her very detailed description of the angel's appearance was deeply impressed on my mind.

The children didn't have toys to play with except for a cricket my older brother caught for them and placed in a box. They enjoyed feeding that cricket and tickling it with a hair so it would sing. Most of the young neighbors and teenagers would swim in the canal or lake, either naked or with all their clothes on. Mom's third daughter would get a floating banana log for them to hold onto teaching the little ones how to swim. Mom, on many occasions, would cook the tiny little fish, without gutting or removing their heads. These were their favorites. Mom always warned them not to choke on the bones.

Mom had a very difficult time finding enough food for her children. Whatever she found she made her children all eat together. These were the times when she would talk very personally with us and share both good and sad stories happening in the world around them. She would never discuss her personal life. We didn't have a table and chairs but would squat on mats, on the ground, around a large wooden bed with the food in the middle. The bed was a five by six foot rectangle of two inch thick wood supported by sixteen inch legs on the four corners. There was no padding on our beds as on the beds available to the rich. The chairs we had in the house were benches with embroidered pillows for comfort. I remember an older lady, the grandma who loved Mom, who would sit with me and enjoy the small stewed fish on cold rice.

When I was about four years old a startling event happened. As I stood by the side of the house overlooking the canal I suddenly saw a bright shining blue shadow pass in front of my eyes. I shouted and told Mom that I had seen an Angel's light. All Mom answered was, "I saw it too".

Hoi came home about this time. He had blisters and sores all over his body. He had been captured by the Viet Minh and tortured as he had been an interpreter for the Japanese who were fighting the Viet Minh. He was very mad at Mom for birthing me. He did not believe Mom's revelation of a virgin birth and thought Mom had been fooling around with another man. This caused them to have a fierce fight. He stayed home until his body sores healed and then was gone again.

In 1951 Hoi returned home again and moved the family to Dalat. There were many papers to fill out to get permission to move and it took several months for approval. After final approval it took three days by bus to reach Dalat. We were searched many times on the road. When settled in Dalat, Hoi remained with us for a few days before leaving saying he had a job some three hours away. Mom found out that he had a mistress in Dalat and that was the reason he moved his family there. Hoi had a child with this woman, a boy, who was three years younger than me. Mom was abused by Hoi every time she mentioned this mistress.

On one occasion Hoi brought his mistress home with their child to show Mom that he had another woman and a child by that woman. Mom was very unhappy and seeing how Hoi pampered this woman became very jealous. Her blood boiling, she cursed the woman and hit her and the woman hit back. Hoi intervened and struck Mom hard enough to break out her remaining front teeth. My brother Nathan tried to stop the fight but he was too small to do anything. He cried and begged his father to stop the fighting. Following that incident Mom became very sick for many months. Hoi never assisted her or demonstrated any concern for her health or provide any care.

There were very few cyclos in Dalat due to the poor roads, steep hills and deep valleys. People either walked or used horses to pull carriages for transportation. The first house we moved into in Dalat was a two story building and we occupied the basement. It was next to an unusual Temple which was actually just a small house. One of their Priests, our neighbor, called to me and passed fruit through the fence for me to eat. I learned that in that Temple they just sat on the ground, worshiping and praying for some unseen ghostly image, to enter the body of another. On one occasion I dreamed that the image appeared. I was afraid and scared and told Mom about this bad appearance. Mom gathered up a long piece of paper covered with red religious words and symbols. She would hold it high while burning incense and recite prayers to calm me by chasing the image away. This was done to make me sleep. She would burn the red paper and mix the ashes with water and force me to drink that mix. I remember this had no immediate effect but I did close my eyes and later fall asleep.

In Dalat Mom received very little support from Hoi even though he was at home more than when living in Can Tho. Mom needed someone to do yard work and to chop wood so she hired a local Montagnard to help. This man, naturally small in stature, could not chop wood as expected. In showing him how to do it, Mom would stand the log on end and with one strike of the axe, split the log in two pieces. He learned very quickly and became very helpful. I still didn't have any toys to play with so I would just walk and run around our building for fun.

There was a man who lived in our building who would give me food or money each time he saw me. On one occasion he lured me into his room, removed my underpants and molested me. I told Mom and she became very mad and brutally attacked the man. I was scolded and directed to never go near that man again. On another occasion the people who lived upstairs threw out smelly fish water as I was passing by and it got all over me. I was covered with fish blood, scales and intestines. This made Mom very mad and she violently accosted the neighbor. She gave me a complete bath but my hair continued to smell like fish.

At another time I began to cough a lot so Mom prepared a solution of Green Snake Lizard and charcoal for me to eat to stop the cough. This did stop the cough. Mom had many natural remedies to cure all ills. There was a time when I continually had a stomach ache. I was not eating much and was becoming very skinny. Hoi brought home chocolate flavored Worm Treatment pills. I liked these pills and ate more than I should have. This caused me to have continuous diarrhea during which I expelled tapeworms. This obviously had been my problem. Following that I no longer had the stomach ache and regained my appetite.

We moved to several homes and during this time Hoi became regularly employed as a teacher. After several months Hoi came down with a paralyzing disease affecting one leg and a part of the other. He remained in the hospital for several months. When released his paralysis affected him so that he could walk only with a cane. He was able to continue work as a teacher. During this time he had been staying at home as his other woman now had a different man.

Hoi was a good teacher, had a very popular personality and was surrounded by many friends. He was loved and admired for his academic skills by teachers from many different schools in the area. During Tet celebration time Hoi always received many gifts from teachers, students and parents. They brought china dishes, wines, liquor, fruit, different foods and even live chickens and ducks.

Hoi became concerned to find a religion for himself. A teacher friend introduced him to the Cao Dai faith. He often went to the Cao Dai Temple, quite far from where we lived. He followed the Cao Dai rules, became a vegetarian to regain his health and become a better man. Unfortunately it was too late. Hoi paid big prices for Chinese and Vietnamese herb medicines to cure his ills but they did little good. His paralysis began to get worse and spread to more of his body. He spent much time in the hospital but continued to teach. During this time he impregnated Mom again with my sister Christine (Nham), born in 1952. Hoi's entire personality changed. He had become very good with children, teaching the older children many languages including French, German and Japanese. He made my brothers and sisters learn French and Japanese at home.

One evening, after Hoi completed teaching my school lessons for the day, a teacher friend came for a chat with him. They talked, ate and drank wine and after a few hours Hoi complained of being sick. The friend went home. Hoi laid down to rest at about 5 PM. At midnight he went to the bathroom and then back to bed complaining that he had a severe headache. Mom called a doctor to the house who after examining him, found that Hoi had burst a vein in his head. Hoi had had a stroke. He could not hear or speak. The next morning many friends and neighbors came to try their techniques of nature to cure him but nothing helped. Around midnight that evening my sister woke me up and told me our dad had died. She said that I must get up and close his eyes. I did touch his face and slowly closed his eyes. Hoi was 43 years old when he died. At Hoi's funeral, many students and teachers from schools from miles around came to walk to the cemetery. Over a thousand people attended. After the first group was at the cemetery, there were still lines of mourners on the ten mile road from the Dalat marketplace.

At this time my youngest sister, Christine, was about 6 months old. Mom had to work hard selling fruits and snacks at the school to support her children and to pay off debts created by Hoi's long illness. It took several years to pay all of Hoi's debts. She continued to work long hours to pay large fees for her children to continue in school, especially for my brother, Nathan, and me.

After all of her children were married or living on their own. Mom lived with me in Vietnam until I left for America. I processed the necessary documents to sponsor Mom to immigrate to the United States. These papers were approved in 1978 but she was afraid to travel alone at that time. She waited until 1989 so she could travel with her daughter-in-law and grandchildren. On arrival in the United States Mom established residence in Southern California.

My brother, Nathan, was able to escape across the Cambodian border and get to the United States. He immediately took extensive training to become a medical technician specializing in the field of working with disabled persons. He was hired to work in a California hospital. His job was in a different city from that where his wife had established residence. Being very successful in his position as a medical technician he did not join her when she requested that he find a different job at her location. This separation eventually ended in divorce. Due mainly to the stress of his divorce

Nathan had several minor vehicle accidents resulting in the suspension of his driver's license. His only transportation to his work site was by bicycle. While riding his bicycle to work one day, he was hit by a car and injured so severely that he could no longer work. Mom cared for him following his injuries.

Tung Thi Ngo, Mom

This became much of a burden for Mom so I moved Mom and Nathan to Guam to live with me. Mom suffered from high blood pressure which I treated by requiring her to adopt proper eating habits. After a year of good nutrition her high blood pressure dissipated and she exhibited good health for her age. During her centennial years, while living at our home In Ocala, Florida, she would be up early in the morning to prepare coffee and get the household moving. For exercise she would take short walks and ride her three wheel bicycle. In her 105th year she lost balance and fell while walking down the hall to her room and broke her left leg in two places. Her injuries were at the hip and ankle. She had to return to the hospital twice and her injuries were slow to heal. Her mind was very sharp but her body began to give up. At the age of 105, while in the hospital, she passed away, not wanting to be a burden to those around her.

After a brief, private service by the seashore, at her request, her cremated remains were presented to the sea. Still living at our home, brother Nathan died two years later at the age of 68. With a final service, the same as that of his mother, Nathan's cremated remains were presented to the sea.

I was very sad and could not share my sadness with anyone until two months later. I expected my Mom to live many more years or at least until I finished my book. I wanted her to be my witness in support of the story of how I was born. I want the world to know this heavenly happening.

TUYET MAI

Following my ethereal birth my Mom gave me the name Tuyet Mai. I have always believed in the mysterious ways of God. When the time comes, the world will know the true story of my Mom and me and our service to God. Most of the stories which I had heard concerning this time in Mom's life had been very secretly held within herself. She did not discuss her personal difficulties with anyone. She did not talk about her position in the Ngo family. She didn't tell anyone that she had been raped very early in her life. She did not tell anyone of the events leading to her godly pregnancy with me and how I was born. She never discussed the life she endured with her husband, Hoi.

Later, I had a vision of her very difficult life and asked her why she had not told anyone of her many difficulties. All she responded was that the details seen in my visions were very true. She said the events were very painful and difficult to tell and hard for others to believe. In 1989, a few months after Mom came to America, I wrote a long letter to my brother, Nathan, and related my vision and Mom's confirmation of past events in her life. He was shocked to learn her story.

Nathan continued to think about Mom's past and when she came to America, he confronted her with these episodes of her past. Mom confirmed that all stories were true. They both were personally physically shivering and shaking during these discussions. Mom never told Nathan that she had been an orphan in the Ngo family.

Following this, Nathan began to ask me more questions about God. During his early lifetime he had been a very faithful follower and preacher of his "no name" religious beliefs. He suddenly rejected this "no name" religion. Those followers of the "no name" religion became upset with me. They accused me of destroying a belief Nathan had followed since High School. They wrote letters to him asking him why he was following the devil. Mom, who also had followed this "no name" religion, withdrew from this belief. In all honesty, I did not try to convince them as to whom they should worship, follow or believe. Nathan knew that there was only one God to worship and follow.

In early 1945, Mom, then pregnant with me, was experiencing the chaotic times of the world around her. The evil political and religious forces at all levels were demonstrating their strength against their lesser foes. Nationally this included the Chinese, French, Japanese and British, each against the other. At the local level the Vietminh, Vietcong, Hoa Hao and Cao Dai were vying for control. Villages were being harassed and particularly by the Hoa Hao who treated everyone who did not follow their belief very brutally. Many, including my family, were thought to be their enemy and were thrown out of their village. Mom was removed from her village with her four other children and me in her womb. When she was finally able to return to her home it had been totally stripped of anything moveable to include food and clothing. Again, Mom had to rebuild her house with some help from my brother.

In September 1945 Mom, at home, began giving birth to me. Four hours later I was delivered by a midwife. Mom had no time to relax and take care of herself. Within two days after my birth, Mom was up very early every morning preparing "Xoi" to sell at the market. Xoi is steamed sweet sticky rice eaten with fresh shredded coconut and sugar or ground peanuts mixed with salt and sugar served on banana leaves. This was usually sold in the early morning for breakfast. Mom carried the Xoi in a large bamboo basket balanced on top of her head or sometimes with a bamboo stick over her shoulder with a basket on each end.

Sometimes she would come home early with food for the day and at other times she could not sell enough Xoi and was very sad not to have enough money to buy food for the day or to buy milk for me as a baby. My sister (the second child) would cook rice and take the juice from the rice, mix with sugar to feed me. Mom would catch fish and shrimp, raise fruit and vegetables and even fry crickets and make cookies, anything to sell to earn money to feed her children.

I grew up in Dalat, a beautiful city in the mountains, where Hoi moved the family in early 1951. At that time I was almost six years old. Hoi died in April 1953. After Hoi died, I was sick for several days with a very high fever. Everyone thought I would die. I stayed home alone. On one occasion when Mom came home she found that I had the measles. She went out and found soy beans and pea pods (dau xang) and cooked them to get the juice. I drank that juice and very soon began to feel better. Mom continued to feed me that juice and the next day the measles disappeared. I have never forgotten the natural herb medicines.

Mom worked very hard selling fruits and snacks to school children to pay the debt and for our schooling. My brother and I helped Mom by carrying baskets of her things to sell at school. My youngest sister, Nham (Christine), was at that time just six months old. A good friend of Mom watched the baby while Mom was selling. I watched my baby sister when I came home from school.

After a while my older brother was accepted by a tailor for training in that trade. My older sister had been accepted for training as an embroiderer at Domain de Marie, a Catholic Convent. My next sister was trained to be a nurse and live at their facility. She was placed in charge of nursing and teaching the older children, toddlers and babies. She lived at the child care facility and every Sunday she would walk with the boarding students to church. She took care of from 25 to 75 patients by herself from 7 AM to 2 PM. She provided medicine and gave shots as needed. The medicines were provided by an international agency at no charge. My oldest brother and sister could not help Mom financially as they made very little pay.

When I was six years old, we continued to live in the Dalat mountain area. During the winter, in heavy rain storms, I would go out on the asphalt street and pick up hail, which I loved to eat mixed with sweet condensed milk. Sometimes the hail was as big as your thumb. I did not have toys to play with except for a doll. Mom bought me a live baby chicken and a baby duck which I raised. My older brother taught me to play hopscotch, walk on stilts, jump rope and to play badminton. Just before summer vacation some of our teachers took our schools on a camping trip. They taught us how to set up our own tents, collect wood and build our own fires. We learned to heat the sand and rocks for cooking. We had contests for who built their tent the fastest and who had the best looking tent.

Mom sent me to a teacher's house for summer school when I was in the third grade. The other children and I would take a short cut through a fruit and vegetable garden to get to the teacher's house. After school we would go the same route home and stop by a little creek which had small fish, shrimp and crabs. We could catch the fish and shrimp in our hat but did not catch the crabs. We were afraid they would bite with their large claws. When I got home my Mom taught me how to catch the crabs without being bitten. The next day we took a little container with us and hid it in the garden before going to class. On the way home we hurried to the creek and caught more fish, shrimp and crabs this time. This was the most fun I had ever had. On one rainy day I was racing with my friends through the garden and fell down a steep slope. My clothes were all muddy. We decided to go to a deep pond, where the farmer got his water, to wash off my dirty clothes. When I tried to stand on a small step ladder I slipped and fell into the pond and I almost drowned. I thought I was going to die. Luckily my friends pulled me out. I was able to get my clothes clean.

I went home and didn't tell my Mom right away about almost drowning. I kept it a secret because I thought if she knew I wouldn't get to play with my friends again. We dug white clay from that creek and formed pots and bowls to cook rice. They didn't work. Mom saw what we had done so she bought us two little clay pots and bowls. She made us some small chop sticks, showed us how to make a fire and cook rice. After catching fish, shrimp and crabs we added vegetables and made soup to eat in our little bowls. We had a lot of fun and enjoyed eating our own cooking.

Mom bought a small chick for me to grow for fun. After several months we had a barn full of large chickens, a rooster and many chicks. I would often watch the hens lay their eggs. Mom would scold me if I watched too close saying that if I bothered the hen the eggs would not come out in a nice shape. Mom liked to eat the egg raw, as soon as it was laid and still warm. Over time we had many chickens which were not penned but roamed over the entire area. When we called they would come to be fed their corn and raw rice. They would nest nearby and go to sleep early. Around four in the morning, before dawn, the rooster would start crowing and the chickens would start their day.

There were two very special events I always remember from my elementary school days. My third grade teacher showed our class how to smoke a plain piece of glass. We did this so we could look through the dark glass and observe the solar eclipse. This teacher also taught us how to fill a bucket with water from the nearby stream and treat it with a purifying pill to make it good to drink.

My sisters helped Mom wash clothes on the week-ends and on the days they were not working. They would either wash clothes at home or at the Cau Ong Dao. This was a creek flowing from the Dam of the Xuan Huong Lake. On one occasion when I went with them to wash clothes I fell in the water again. This time it wasn't as bad as the last slip from the ladder. This creek was also a source of water for the local gardeners. They would carry two buckets, one at each end of a long pole, fill the buckets by dumping each end in the water and trot that water to the field to cover their garden rows. This was repeated many times.

My brother, Nathan, learned to swim in this creek. On one occasion a friend held Nathan's head under water as if trying to drown him. Nathan had to bite the boy's leg to get released. My oldest brother and Nathan often fished in Xuan Huong Lake. In the evening they would place their short poles, set up with lines holding many hooks, along the lake bank. They would check the lines early the next morning and often find many fish. It was a lot of fun to go out with them in the morning and see many swimming fish attached to the hooks. We would always take home a large bucket of fish of many different sizes.

One night my oldest brother brought a lady, Chi Nam, home from his work place and asked Mom to let her stay with us for a short while. Mom said she could stay with us for a month or until she could find a job. On a following afternoon, after I helped Mom bring all the selling items back home, I sat down to sort a basket of pears. I had my baby sister's cradle next to me. I began sorting the good and bad pears and asked Chi Nam if she would like to eat some pears. In a very strange manner, right away she took a spare knife and cut out the good and bad parts of several pears and ate them. After eating she took the knife and again in a very strange manner chopped up the basket with the knife. I asked her to stop but she kept chopping. She then said she was tired and went to bed. When Mom came home from shopping for things to sell the next day, she cooked and fed us and gave Chi Nam food to eat. Chi Nam ate and ate, just stuffing food in her mouth and kept asking for more. When Mom wouldn't give her any more Chi Nam continued to beg in many different and strange voices. She cried and again begged for food.

Mom felt that something unknown had gotten into Chi Nam's body. Mom got very mad and shouted at her. In the beginning she only wanted to help this poor lady. I heard Mom ask her why she had come to bother us. Mom directed her to leave our house. Chi Nam cried and then laughed in tones that scared me. Mom explained to me that every time the devil got into her body Chi Nam spoke with a different voice and had different actions. No one could stop them but Mom and me. Using a big iron chain from the rear of the landlord's house, like those to pull a tractor, Mom would slam it down on the floor making a horrible noise. Mom explained to me that the noise would scare the devil away.

Following this episode Chi Nam did not remember anything. I asked her why she cursed and laughed terribly and she said she didn't remember what had taken place. Chi Nam asked, "What is wrong with me"? There was a day, when I was home alone with my baby sister and Chi Nam, the devil got into Chi Nam again and she began her crazy actions. I was not afraid of her. I stopped her crazy actions by pointing my finger directly into her face and saying, "Stop! Whoever is there get out of this lady" and It stopped right away due to my pointing.

On one occasion Chi Nam said to me she wanted to go to the bathroom. The bathroom was outside and I was too small to lead her. I asked two neighbor ladies to lead her. Halfway there, Chi Nam became very strangely physical and fought the ladies. They couldn't control her. I again pointed my finger at Chi Nam and said, "Whoever is in this lady better get out now". Chi Nam immediately stopped her fighting. The Devil had immediately left Chi Nam's body. The ladies stared at me in fear wondering why the Devil responded to my command.

After this event Chi Nam asked why all three of the ladies were around her and why I was there. I told her what had happened. I began to realize that there were special powers within me. Chi Nam remained calm for about a week but later her crazy actions continued. My sister brought holy water home from the Catholic Church. She would dip flowers into this water and sprinkle it on Chi Nam during her crazy actions. This did not calm her down. I saw Mom curse and threaten Chi Nam's demons demanding that they not bother Chi Nam. Mom addressed the demons saying we are good people only trying to help this homeless lady. About a week later Chi Nam had remained calm during this time and Mom gave her some money, asked her to leave our home. She departed.

When I was nine years old I was introduced to the "Foster Parents Association", sponsored by the United States. Through correspondence I became the child of Foster Parents from the United States. By the time I was eleven years old I had been assigned to three different Foster Parents. I went with Mom to the Foster Parents Association office once every month and I was given 500 Piaster. They also gave me many types of household necessities. The allowance was increased every two years and by the time the program terminated I was receiving 1,200 Piaster monthly. This was a great help to Mom.

I taught my little sister Nham "Christine", the favorite dance of our culture when she was four years old. She was very cute and a very good dancer. She performed her dance every time we had foreign guests. We would always receive little gifts or money from them. The Catholic Sisters, my older sister's worked for, asked me to train a group of eight or ten children to dance and perform at their facility, Domain de Marie. I gathered some village children and taught them the cultural dances. Christine filled in the group as an angel. Their performances were very successful and the children received many rewards from the Sisters of the Domain de Marie Convent.

The word of their delightful performances spread around the villages and they soon were invited to perform in the big local theatre with over 1000 persons in the audience. The children danced and I sang behind the curtain. While the children danced, Christine came on the stage to do her part and the audience thought that she was just lost. After a few minutes of her talented performance they began to clap and throw money on the stage for her. They did three dances that night and collected over 1,000 Piaster. They gave Christine the name of Xuan Huong (the name of Dalat's lake). This group which included Christine, neighbor children, classmates and I, continued to perform for the surrounding villages just for fun.

Occasionally I would walk with Christine to visit our older sister, some fifteen miles away from our home. Our older sister would give us money to buy noodles or sweets. One day I rode a bicycle with Christine to our second sister's home in Domain de Marie. While peddling down a steep slope a large water truck approached very fast from our right side. It was apparent that he wasn't going to stop. A lady selling things by the side of the road saw the truck heading for us and yelled to warn us. That warning allowed us to be missed and probably saved our lives. When Christine was big enough to walk to school by herself, she would always take something to eat. Mom would always try to stop her when she ate too much. One day she kept asking Mom for sweets so much that she made Mom so mad that she threw the knife she was using to cut pineapple, at Christine. Christine was cut and bleeding and ran to a neighbor for help.

Quite often I would take Christine to carnivals and fun festivals. On one occasion I took her to a movie. Christine went to the same Catholic High School which my brother, Nathan, and I attended. Nathan and I were good students and were designated for full scholarships several times. For this we received big prizes at the end of the school year. Even though I was a good student I was slapped with a ruler on the palm of my hand many times. I was left handed and the teacher wanted me to write with my right hand. I also remember being punished for talking too much with the student next to me. The teacher would make me kneel down on a prickly Jack Fruit for almost an hour. At the end of my punishment my knees were always bruised and bleeding from the Jack Fruit spikes. Regardless, at the end of the school year I was selected as the best student of the entire school and was awarded a one week trip to Nha Trang.

One student from each elementary school in the highlands was selected for the trip. I was surprised to be met by our Mayor before getting on the train to Nha Trang. On getting off the train we were met by the Nha Trang Mayor and other high ranking persons and teachers of the area. I felt very special then and even now it remains an event which I have never forgotten.

Mom received permission to set up a small locked wheel cabinet under a shed at the Catholic high school. Here she and Nathan could sell snacks at recess. Later on I helped them sell. We received awards for being helpful students. It was very hard for Mom to put money together for our tuition fees each month but she wanted us to remain in the Catholic High School.

Mom heard good stories from our neighbors that Grand Lycee (French High School) was a good place to sell snacks to students. Mom decided to send me to school at Grand Lycee so in addition to classes I could sell snacks to students there. My French language was weak so I had to take French courses at night at Petite Lycee. I remained in classes at Grand Lycee for a few months but because it was so far from home and the tuition was very high, which Mom could not afford to pay, I returned to the Catholic High School.

I normally tried to dress neatly but all I had were old and worn Western World style clothes. I had a few Vietnamese clothes but they looked like plain pajamas. The few pretty dresses I had my sister had given me. Those had been given to her by one of her friends. That friend was the daughter of a Frenchman and she had very nice things. On occasion, when walking home and wearing one of the nice dresses, I would be followed and flirted with by young Cadets from the Dalat Military

Officers Academy. When I was near my home I would stop at a neighbor's house that had a store upstairs, and tell the Cadets I was home. I hoped that then they would stop following me. I did not want them to see the rather poor home where I lived.

During this time Mom began to get sick, very often lasting for weeks at a time, and she could not do her selling. I had to take days off from school to sell during her sick times. I got behind in my school work having difficulty keeping up with my studies. We encouraged Mom to discontinue selling at the schools. To help, Nathan and I followed friends and neighbors to the forests to collect wood to sell. I did some work on the side. Nathan and I continued to sell snacks at the school and at sport stadiums on weekends. This was during the time when I was still receiving support from the United States Foster Parents.

Nathan went to the forest, very early in the morning, with neighbor's maids, arriving back home after four in the afternoon. He would have wood in racks which he carried on his shoulders padded with a jacket to keep from getting sore. The wood looked very nice. Mom was very surprised that Nathan could chop it so neat and evenly since this was the first time he had done this kind of work. Nathan did tell Mom that he did not do the chopping as a nice man helped him with the wood. When it was time to come home the man saw that Nathan did not have much in his carrier so the man helped him chop more and also gave him some of his wood. Nathan said it was hard work but after a few weekends he learned well and produced a lot of nicely cut wood.

I asked Mom to let me go to the forest with Nathan and she let me go. Early on a Saturday morning we went to the forest with ten other people. I couldn't believe it was so far to walk. At that time I was fifteen years old. We walked almost two hours to where the group thought we would find the type wood they wanted. It was a very thick forest. I was not afraid of the wild animals but very fearful of leaches. I carried a machete and wood racks with sticks to prop up the racks. We always took a small lunch and water with us. These woods had many types of wild animals. I was told by a friend that if you see a Tiger make a loud noise by banging the machete on your canteen and it will scare the animal away.

I had only a little training from my brother on how to find the right dry wood and how to chop each piece to the proper size. Everyone went their own way going deep in the forest to find the type of wood best to chop. Chopping was very difficult and it was also difficult to load the wood on to my carrying pack so it wouldn't fall off as I carried it home. My friends always helped me get my pack loaded. While carrying the chopped logs, the long walk home seemed twice as far as the trip out.

The forest was very pretty and the air was clear to breathe. The noise of the water running in the creek, the tweeting of the birds and the clicking of the crickets gave me a very peaceful, special feeling. I felt I was special and these surroundings helped me understand all the good and bad things I had endured as a younger child. The walk home was very difficult. My shoulders and feet became very sore. It was such a relief when I finally reached home. I prayed to God thanking him for the special day and the beautiful, natural things I had learned about life.

The next day a friend asked me to go again. I did not want to go but thinking about our need for money I agreed to go again. During the dry season friends taught me how to look for dead dry trees to chop down for wood. We were told to call for help if the tree was too large. We found a tree which, by using a rope and our machete, we chopped down without calling for help. I had learned to use a rope and tie knots the Scout way. We chopped the tree into small pieces and carried it home as before.

After a while I became accustomed to this work and through the Summer time we made enough money for our school tuition. There were more funds needed for our daily living. Besides collecting wood we would go to the stadiums and other big gathering areas to sell snacks. We usually sold out what we had to sell. We received a lot of tip money and gave it all to Mom. I also rolled cigarettes by hand and cut sewing patterns for business owners to earn some money. When I was very young it was difficult for me to do the things required to help Mom but I was smart enough to handle difficult situations. I often prayed and cried because I had to work so hard. We were very poor and I had no time for fun. I did feel that I was always very close to God.

My Mom, in the beginning, was an ancestor worshiper. She would go to a Temple where they worshipped many paper idols. They had many different types of incense and the priests would spray the idols for luck. I did not like this as she spent much money there. As I have noted before, she would go to the Temple every time she felt sick to get a piece of paper with unintelligible script. She would burn that paper, dissolve the ashes in a glass of water, and drink it. The more she drank the sicker she would get. She would talk to herself a lot and shout loud that the devil had come to get her. Usually my brother and I would calm her down and pray to God to chase this problem from her.

Each time we moved to a new house Mom would find a small space to set up an altar with two nice red candles, incense and a picture of Hoi. Each day Mom would find time to sit or kneel down in front of the altar and pray for good days to come. She would direct me to participate in her ritual. Once in a while I would follow her instruction just to please her. Most of the time I would find some reason not to perform as she did as I did not believe in praying as Mom prayed. One day she placed a tray of many types of fruit on Hoi's altar. She explained that the day was the anniversary of his death and that she should worship him and leave many different foods for him by the altar. On one occasion I had a very clear vision of Hoi standing by the door, dressed as I remembered him as a teacher. I asked this vision, "Are you Hoi?" and it answered, "Yes". Following this the same face appeared on the altar. I asked the vision who he was and it answered, "Hoi". I told Mom of this occurrence and she did not believe me. I read this as a sign that Mom must end the worshiping as it was ruining her life.

On one occasion Mom took me to a Temple and showed me the Priests, men and women squatting in front of a colorful altar. They were dressed in very bright clothing with red or black cloth covering their heads and faces. For ten or fifteen minutes their heads would spin. They would then lift their veils and identify themselves as angels or fairies. Mom told me that when their heads were spinning that is when angels and fairies enter the body and heel sick persons.

Mom forced me to do the same as the priests. I complied just to please her and to test what was happening. Unfortunately, after following their procedures for more than thirty minutes, nothing happened. I was trying to understand if this was all true.

Mom went back to selling again for almost a year and then became sick again. I filled in for Mom for more than two weeks but she continued to get sick. I decided with Mom that I should stop going to school in the day time. I would do the selling in the daytime and go to school at night. I did very well at selling. My brother and I would go to the market very early in the morning to buy merchandise and then hurry to get things set up before the students would come to school. Frequently, early in the morning, I did not have enough money to buy enough goods to last the whole day. On many occasions I would have to go back to the market two or three times during the day to replenish our goods with funds from our sales.

After a while I was able to save enough money to buy shoes and clothes for me and my younger sister. There was a Western dress that I wanted for my sister but it was too expensive. I decided to buy the material and make that dress for her for Tet. I drew and cut out a pattern for the dress that I had seen in the clothing shop at the market. I drew the dress style on newspaper and attempted to make it by myself. I had never made a dress before. Mom was worried that I would ruin the good material. After a long night of sewing by hand it turned out very nice in time to be Christine's Tet gift.

After a year Mom became well again and took over the selling and I was able to return to day time school. My oldest brother got married as did my second sister. My third sister (Cuc) decided to be a Nun. She was admitted to the convent but after a while became discontent due to misunderstandings and differences in beliefs in the convent. She withdrew from the convent and very soon she started teaching at a French school. She contributed her pay to Mom for food. She demanded that Mom buy only good food products so to get good value for her contributions. The funds she provided were very little compared to what I gave Mom. Cuc's attitude toward the family was somewhat selfish.

For several years Mom and I were the sole sellers of snacks at the schools. In later years the schools allowed others to sell and it became very hard for us to earn the needed money. My brother and I had to teach small classes at night to earn more funds. Also I continued to receive funds from my foster parents in the United States which helped a lot. During that time I was still organizing and managing the dancing group which performed at Convent des Oiseaux, Domaine de Mary Convent and other Catholic organizations and other villages. We all earned generous tips at these performances which helped family finances.

In school I chose my first language to learn to be French and the second language, English. At that time the United States military had become established in Vietnam. Military Chaplains and other preachers from America and Australia were there. I went to their services not only to hear the Gospel but to learn English. I found that I was learning English faster there than just taking a few hours of English classes at school. I concentrated hard to learn English so I would be able to work for the Americans later.

I attended meetings with United States Missionaries who were very nice and spoke English slowly for me to understand. I was able to answer some of their questions but those I could not answer I would write down. When at home I would look up the meaning of the words in my dictionary and make sentences for my answers to the Missionaries at our next meeting. I kept doing that for several months. I also wrote letters, in English, to Missionaries in other countries. I had help from a friend to correct my grammar in my writings. This was very helpful and at school I became a student that could speak English better than anyone else in the class. My brother Nathan could speak English better than me and he would help the Missionaries with their translation of the Vietnamese language as they preached the Gospel of God. Meanwhile the Missionaries were also learning the Vietnamese language.

As time passed Mom got sick again and could not sell any more. Nathan decided to go to work for the Americans to help our family. He obtained a job as an Interpreter and translator for the USOM (United States Operations Mission). He was assigned to be an interpreter for a USOM Advisor travelling from Dalat to Dam Pao farm near the hospital. That hospital was established by US Advisors who worked with the local doctors teaching nursing skills. Nathan and his advisor boss taught the locals how to raise pigs and chickens and develop better farming practices. The hospital had more than twenty doctors and nurses and my brother encouraged me to go there and learn nursing. I told him I would go in the summer after finishing school. Unfortunately, after a few months I was very sick.

At this time my sister, who was a devout Catholic, was very upset that my brother and I were going to the meetings of the Protestant missionaries. She scolded me and even hit me trying to stop me from going to the meetings. I became so depressed that it affected my heart and my nervous system. I was admitted to the hospital in Dalat for several weeks and then taken to Saigon for treatment to include my treatment for neurosis. I almost died at this time as I was also found to have Skreys White Measles. I was taken on a litter to be examined by a doctor. He explained that it was good that he was consulted otherwise I may have died.

For my treatment I was prescribed to receive shots daily for two weeks. These shots were to be given into my veins by a nurse at home or by going to the doctor's office. There were only two days during the week that the nurse could come to my friend's house in Saigon to give me the shots. My family arranged for a preacher friend of the family to give me my shots. He said he knew the procedure but it resulted that he did not give the shot correctly. The shot into my hip area was not done properly and caused much pain and an abscess was created which swelled into the size of a small ball. I was sent to the Free Hospital where I was admitted to have the abscess removed. The operation was very painful as it was done without an anesthetic.

After the operation I moved to my older brother's house in Saigon, which was very far from the hospital. After the second checkup at the hospital I decided to change my bandages myself. I would use a whole roll of bandage for my wound which was three inches deep.

It was very painful but I healed well. After healing I decided to return to Dalat. When I returned home my brother Nathan took me to Dam Pao Hospital where he worked. I had the opportunity to meet many doctors and nurses there. I found that I could have gone to their hospital for treatment instead of going to Saigon. The doctors invited me to stay with the American nurses while I visited there.

I went to the Dam Pao Hospital with a friend from the Convent school. I was taught nursing skills and helped as an interpreter for the doctors. My friend was able to practice her English. We continued to go to the Dam Pao Hospital each time we had time off from school. The missionary nurses were great. We ate with the doctors and nurses and slept in the nurse's quarters. I asked Mom if I could work there and become a nurse. She did not approve. She wanted me to continue my education and work in the same province as Dalat not far away in Lam Dong where Dam Pao Hospital was located.

During this time the fighting with the Viet Cong was becoming more intense and there was more American presence in Vietnam. There were frequent communist raids on isolated areas and Vietnamese, working for the Americans, were primary targets for assassination.

My brother Nathan, after working for USOM for several years, decided he wanted to become a preacher to be a servant of God. He wanted to introduce me to work for USAID (United States Agency for International Development), created by President Kennedy in 1961, which absorbed USOM. They had an opening for a typist for the boss of his boss. I did not know how to type so Nathan purchased a typewriter and taught me to type at home. My fastest speed became thirty-five words per minute. At that time my English was good enough to go to work for the Americans. In July, 1966, even though I could barely type, I was hired as a typist by USAID to work for the National Police Field Force Advisors. I was paid 6,000 Piaster a month, the same pay as my brother.

After a week I was assigned as an Interpreter and Translator. At that time there were about 200 Vietnamese workers and contractors working for the Police Field Force Advisors. They were paid on the American wage scale to work for the Vietnamese Police Department. I translated several important documents and messages for both the Vietnamese National Field Force and the American Advisors as they went on operations to look for the enemy. I was the only lady interpreter in the Administrative office for both the Vietnamese National Field Force and the American Advisors in the Administrative office. I had a lot of work from typing, interpreting, doing the payroll, and book-keeping to help the American Advisors.

In the administrative office I had one old boss responsible for the payroll and bookkeeping, balancing the funds and payroll. He had a hard time keeping up with the workload and when he made mistakes it would take him a long time to find what he had done wrong. I offered to help him but he rarely accepted help. In addition to my regular duties and after being tested by the Senior Boss, I successfully completed the payroll and financial work. I completed the work accurately and on time and had no problem balancing a million Piaster budget. Within six weeks my salary was increased from 6,000 to 9,000 Piaster a month. During this time I found that the foremen and time keepers were cheating, falsifying the hours they had worked on their time cards. The Vietnamese and French contractors were reporting figures much higher than delivered on their invoices for wood, sand and rock. I reported this to my immediate supervisor but as I was too busy to follow up my findings, the problem was never corrected. I worked in that job for over two years.

My workplace was too far to travel each day. It took me two hours daily, by bus, to get to work. I requested that I be transferred to a USAID job in Dalat. The USAID Personnel Advisor accepted me to work in Dalat but I had to wait for a job opening. Mr. Gwynn, who was the Advisor to the National Police Field Force offered to give me a ride to work each day if I would teach him to speak Vietnamese. Every other night he would come to my house for lessons. We had to use kerosene lamps and candles for light. One night he was sitting across from me and I could tell he was not interested in studying. During the teaching I became very attracted to him. That evening he asked me to come beside him. He wanted to give me a hug. When he hugged me, apparently he had ejaculated sperm through his pants. This scared me and I pushed him away. I did not tell these details to Mom. Mom thought that I had sexual intercourse with him. I was a virgin.

After that experience I asked Mr. Gwynn not to come to my house for Vietnamese lessons. I told him that I would come to his office, from time to time, to teach. On several occasions he invited me to have lunch or dinner with the other Advisors. In the large house where the Advisors lived was a sitting room, dining room and kitchen and each Advisor had his own private bedroom. I would usually go to Mr. Gwynn's room to give him his Vietnamese lessons. There was never any sexual contact. On one occasion their Vietnamese cook served us lunch and we went to his room. Later the cook came to the door and asked what we were doing. I responded that I was teaching him Vietnamese. Following that she spread false stories saying that I was being intimate with Mr. Gwynn. Truthfully, I was never intimate with him. I knew he was married and his wife was living in Hong Kong.

One of the Australian Advisors, for whom I worked, brought me bras and under wear on his return from a trip to Hong Kong. When I showed these things to Mom she wanted to know what I had done with him to get these gifts. I told her the gifts were his way of thanking me for my work. There was another time when this Advisor asked me to decorate a Christmas tree and wrap gifts. I helped him for almost two hours until my back was sore. He suggested that I lie down on his bed and relax. I had my hair rolled up so it became a little fuzzy. After I rested we went out to the dining room for a drink. The maid came to me and said you have been in his room for over two hours and your hair is all messed up. "What have you been doing?" I told her we were wrapping Christmas gifts. Her response was, "Really". After this, again many false stories were spread about me being intimate with Mr. Gwynn and the other Advisors.

During this time the Viet Cong had attacked several places, some near my house in the countryside outside the main town of Dalat. They would creep into the area at night and break into houses looking for their adversaries, such as soldiers at home alone, locals working for the South Vietnamese government and locals working for the Americans. Mom feared for my life working as a translator for the Americans. She felt that I needed to find a place to be safe at night. I decided to stay at my girl friend's house which was near the Dalat main streets, hotels and offices. After being there for a week my friend became afraid for her family because I was there. I did not know where to go and what to do. I decided to return home and hope that I would not be caught in our insecure area. Knowing I was trying to get a position in Dalat and might soon leave, my boss asked me to help find someone with strong abilities, as I had demonstrated, to take over my job. I introduced my friend to the Trai Mat Advisor team. Her English was weak and she had few administrative skills but she was the best available and was accepted anyway. I introduced two more girls with similar background and they were also accepted to work.

I went to see the USAID Administrator and Personnel Director and asked for a transfer as soon as possible. Within two days he decided to hire me. He had no immediate position openings but asked me to wait for something to be available. After a month I was accepted to work in Dalat. Now I could walk to work without any problems. My initial job was in the Radio Communications Department. I received only ten minutes training for my position which gave me contact with many radio stations throughout Vietnam. I successfully operated in this job after only four days. It was good to learn and talk to many other people. Later, I was assigned to work with United States Advisors in the Public Works Department. These engineers were working projects in the Central Highlands. My wages were increased to 12,000 Piaster per month. I worked for USMAC (United States Mission Advisors Corps of Engineers), advising the military and civilians responsible for improving roads, building bridges and handling heavy equipment.

My brother, Nathan, took a job as a translator with the United States Intelligence Agency in Dalat which was closer to home. He was receiving 5,000 Piaster a month. After five months he resigned his job and became a servant of God. He worked in Saigon for a short time and then transferred to Pleiku with another religious companion. Nathan soon became disenchanted working with this friend. He became ashamed of the doctrine his friend preached and found he was not honest in his actions. He very soon left this group, which were alien to his own beliefs. My third sister worked for about four months for MACV as a clerk typist. Her job was soon terminated due to poor performance. I became the only one working and providing support to my family. During this time I provided funds for my youngest sister to attend a private Catholic school.

After several months working in the Public Works Heavy Equipment Office I was assigned to the Public Works Chief Engineer's office. A male co-worker and I worked for the Vietnamese Chief Engineer while waiting for the American Engineer Advisor. After a few weeks, just before going home one evening, the new Advisor arrived, shook my hand and said he would return in a few weeks after getting settled in his transfer from Nha Trang. He returned in a few weeks and I finally started working for my new boss. His name was William "Bill" Wann. I worked for him for a week and he had to go away again. He was in charge of the Central Highlands

Public Works Advisors. My job performance was very good as the requirements were not as heavy and did not require the skills as that in Trai Mat. I liked the challenges in addition to interpreting and translating.

During TET of 1968 there was a heavy attack by the Viet Cong hitting many places in Dalat. My brother-in-law, the husband of my second sister, was killed at the gate of Domain de Marie. He was in his military uniform reporting for work. At that time he and his wife had five children and she was pregnant. She was not earning enough to take care of the children and asked me for help. They all moved into my house, now with nine people and a new baby to care for.

I went to work every day constantly worried and afraid of being killed by the Vietcong. They continued to isolate and murder those who worked for the Americans. In March of 1968 my boss, Bill Wann, returned from his inspection trip. In the office he saw that some of our windows had been broken by gun fire and an area of the building had been burned. He was concerned that my family and I were not safe. I told him about my fears, my sister's loss of her husband and that they were all living in my house. When I told him I had no other safe place to live he offered to let me live at his house with two other Advisors. He told me he had guards and the entire upstairs was open for me to stay if I wanted. I told my Mom and sister about the offer and they advised me to accept the offer.

I decided to move into Bill Wann's villa. For safety and security reasons Bill moved his office to the Vietnamese government offices. This was temporary until the security situation improved. Bill was very nice to me. He did not charge me room and board and gave me money to help my family. After a few months he told me that he was separated from his wife and was getting a divorce. Soon he said he wanted to be more than a friend to me. He said he wished to marry me as soon as his divorce was final, which should be automatic in a few months, and after he received the divorce papers.

Bill was very generous and protective of my family and me. I grew to love him very much. I asked Mom's permission to marry Bill and she approved. She said that I must have an engagement ceremony. In June of 1968 we had the engagement ceremony in Dalat. Bill said the wedding would be in Nha Trang. After several months I asked Bill when I could schedule the wedding ceremony. He said that the divorce had not been finalized and we must wait to be legally married. I did not know the American legal requirements so I agreed to wait.

We moved to a better villa which had five bedrooms. Two military advisors and a civilian advisor shared the villa with us. I worked and continued to school to complete courses for graduation. The Public Works Advisors worked together with USAID and MACV. Time went by and Bill made no mention of our marriage date. In July, 1968 Bill told me he had to go to Nigeria in August to instruct the Nigerians on how to install central city generators and to assist in building a power plant. During that time the other officers took me to work and to other places I needed to go. I remained in the Villa with the other officers. A Vietnamese maid worked for us, cleaning the apartments, cooking and washing a lot of clothes by hand daily. During that time I saw several letters for Bill from his wife being held by the other advisor. I felt very sad and it was difficult for me waiting to talk to Bill about the letters.

In early November Bill returned to Vietnam. I was very happy to have him home and anxious to talk to him about the letters. I also wanted to make the decision about when we would get married. In about a week we talked about the wedding and he told me the divorce with his wife had not been completed. He was extremely upset. He remained there with me through November and then told me he had to go to the United States for a while. He told me to remain at the Villa until his return. He showed me where he kept a small pistol and how to use it if I had any difficulties. He was concerned that several young officers may stay at the Villa for a while. I told Bill I would stay with my Mom and come back to check the Villa from time to time. Bill left for the United States in early December, 1968 and left me some money which did not last very long.

I stayed with Mom and kept one room for myself. The remainder of the family lived though out the house. I walked six miles, each way, to work each day. I didn't go out with others or party with other men as I was dedicated to Bill. At the end of the third week of January I went to sleep late. Everyone else in the family was asleep. As I was praying and going to sleep, when I was about to sleep, I had a vision of a man with a long beard. He looked like a Chinese God with angels hovering around him. I walked slowly on a red carpet toward him. He offered two different fruits like apples and pears. He asked me to take the fruit and I asked why. I didn't want to take them.

Then, in my vision, I saw an Angel who came to me with flowers and insisted that I take the fruit. I was told that I was a chosen one, not to be afraid. After that I could not get to sleep and could not understand what it meant. I told the whole story to my Mom. She said the fruit and flowers meant good things would happen. She said it could be a sign that I was going to have a baby. I told Mom that I didn't think that was possible as I had been taking birth control pills while with Bill and had just stopped taking the pills this month. I had a menstrual period just a few days after he left for the United States. Also he had told me that he had his tubes tied so how could I be having his baby. After the vision of that night I was sure I was pregnant. I was surprised and could not understand my pregnancy as I had not had any morning sickness.

Bill returned from the United States at the end of February, 1969. I was very happy to have him back in Vietnam but very worried to tell him that I was pregnant. After a few days I told him I was pregnant and his response was, "Are you joking?" I said no and he felt my stomach. He was very angry and asked me who had I been sleeping with? I told him that I had slept with no one. He then asked, "then how are you pregnant?" I told him the same thing I had told my Mom. Bill said the only way this could happen was that I was fooling around with someone else while he was gone. I could not argue anymore so I just walked away to think about what Bill was thinking and his accusations to me.

A few days later Bill, again angry, came to me and said he had had his sperm tested and the results were negative. He again asked me who I had been sleeping with. I told him again that I had not had sexual intercourse with any man. He did not believe me. I wanted to kill him. I went to the kitchen and grabbed the biggest knife I could find. The cook was there and shouted loudly at me not to use it. She tried to take the knife away from me. Bill saw the knife in my hand and stopped me. He did not shout angrily any more. I told him I would rather go to jail than being accused of lying. I repeated that I had not had sexual intercourse with anyone except him. From that day on he did not repeat his accusations. He quietly counted the days when I was to give birth. When the time came he said it had not been nine months yet and the baby was not his. He did not know that I was having twins. Bill made excuses not to be in the hospital with me. He said he had to go to Nha Trang to supervise a project.

After almost a week with light labor pains I would walk back and forth to my house, three miles each way, constantly trying to push my baby to drop. I kept waiting and waiting and it would not happen. The French doctor decided to prepare me for a Caesarean Section birth. An x-ray confirmed that I was having twins. Blood tests were taken and they prepared me for the operation to be the next day. A Catholic sister begged the doctor to wait as I was so young and this was my first delivery. She asked him to wait two more days and that she would give me medication to help for a natural delivery. She told the doctor that if I was still not ready she would bring me in for the Caesarean Section.

Within two days I was ready. Bill was still in Nha Trang. I gave natural birth to twins. My son, Daniel, came out breach and his body was black and blue. My sister and the mid-wife were afraid that he would not live. After about twelve minutes my daughter, Cathy, delivered normally and was in good condition. I had to have over twenty stitches following the deliveries. The mid-wife prayed and worked on Daniel. My sister cried. The doctor was not there but the mid-wife and the nurses continued to do their best to save Daniel. After several hours he finally began to open his eyes and some ten hours later he began to cry. Daniel weighed 2.3 kilograms and Cathy weighed 2.6 kilograms. They were premature being born after just about seven months of my pregnancy. They remained in incubators for three more weeks.

All my bosses and friends came to the hospital to see me and the babies. Bill did not come until three weeks later to take us home from the hospital. My sister watched the babies while I went back to work during the day and I took care of my babies at night. Bill slept in a different room. I always would bottle feed the twins, once before putting them down for the night. I did not feed them again during the night even if they cried. At first they would cry after feeding but they got used to my way of feeding and soon slept through the night. My Mom and youngest sister remained with us in the Villa for a couple of weeks. Cathy became very sick with appendicitis which caused her intestines to swell up every time she cried. She was checked by the Vietnamese and American doctors. They concluded that her intestines and spleen were premature and that she should be normal as she gets older.

Daniel was often sick with high fever but not seriously ill. My second sister came to our villa every day to watch the twins and wash their clothes. I moved Mom and my youngest sister to our villa to take care of the twins while my second sister was not at home. When the Chief Engineer came to visit us I told him the babies were often sick. He told me, in a very strange way, that I had to make a "marriage ceremony" for them otherwise they would die before they were a year old. He said they were attached in their previous life and have been reincarnated for their current life on earth. I laughed at him and told him I did not believe in reincarnation, especially my children.

The Advisors living in our villa loved my twins and had fun playing with them and enjoyed taking care of them when they had free time. Bill did not do that. He held them and fed them just a few times a week. On one occasion while I was giving the twins a bath, one by one in a little plastic tub, I had to wash their faces with a soft wash cloth. Bill did not see the soap I was using. He told me that I was not bathing them properly, that I must use soap. I showed him that I had already used soap and had poured some oil in the tubs. He did not believe me and brought me a bar of soap and said, "Use it!". I had to use cloth diapers for the twins as paper disposable diapers were not available. The twins had no hair for over a year. Cathy began to walk at nine months but Daniel did not start to walk until he was fourteen months old.

Bill began to avoid being with me. Unknown to me he was quietly arranging for our babies to be adopted. One day an older American couple, around fifty years old, came for a visit and stayed at our Villa. They would take turns holding and feeding the babies, also changing their diapers, singing to them and rocking them to sleep. I asked Bill why they were paying so much attention to the babies. He responded that they had come to Vietnam to adopt them. I was extremely shocked to hear that and asked who had told them they could have our children. He said he had done that so we would not have a problem with the children. Also he said they would give me a lot of money for me and my family. I strongly told him that he had no right to do such a thing. I was extremely mad and told him I would not sell our children for any amount of money. I told him that if he didn't want to raise them I would raise them by myself. I felt that I had enough knowledge and experience to work and care for them. He told me that he felt I could not raise the children properly. He said that I would not be able to get a job if he was not around. He had forgotten that I had my job with USAID before I met him. When the children were two years old Bill was transferred to Suoi Lo O Public Works in Saigon. This was their largest engineering facility in Vietnam. He became an Engineering Executive Advisor. Bill moved us out of the Villa and rented a smaller Villa for us in a different area.

During this time my daughter, Cathy, was very sick. A Vietnamese doctor, using x-ray diagnosis, determined that my daughter had a problem with her spleen. He explained the problem to a doctor in Dalat who arranged to have her flown to the hospital in Cam Ranh Bay. From there she was taken to the 3rd Field Children's Hospital in Saigon. There they found no major problem in her body. I was very pleased to hear that. Son, Daniel, had convulsions several times. I learned that his previous illnesses and high fever were due to tonsillitis. Bill and a friend drove from Saigon to Dalat for the twins second birthday.

This was the time that my brother, Nathan, had resigned from his missionary duties in Pleiku due to conflicts with his co-preacher. He returned to Dalat University for courses to earn his degree. Nathan was selected to attend the Thu Duc Military Officer Academy. Following training he was commissioned as a South Vietnamese Army Lieutenant. He met and married his girl friend in January, 1972. Unfortunately Nathan was seriously injured during a bombing while he commanded troops in Laos. He was wounded by shell fragments that went through his neck and back. After a full day and night alone in the field a helicopter spotted him, picked him up and transported him to a hospital in Saigon. This was just a short time after he was married.

In late 1971 we moved to Saigon to live with Bill. Bill was living in a building rented by USAID with apartments for American advisors. I had to rent a different apartment for Mom, my sister and the children. Bill always gave me a hard time when I took the children to see him. He was afraid a high ranking U.S Embassy lady would see them and cause a problem with his position. We argued a lot. Bill always complained about working with the Vietnamese Engineering Boss. He found that the warehouse inventory was always short, especially with heavy equipment. The Boss could never give an explanation for the losses. Bill was sure the items were stolen.

Bill decided to resign his job in Vietnam and return to the United States. He was sad most of the time. He smoked a lot and drank heavily. Bill never told me but I found out from the military hospital that he had lung cancer. He told me to look for a house to buy. I found a house in Saigon for 800,000 Piaster which he bought and we moved in. In April, 1972, Bill left me for America. He gave me 50,000 Piaster and promised to send me money every month through his friend. The

50,000 Piaster didn't last very long. When my older sister learned that I had a house in Saigon, she and her six children moved in with me. She worked at the Saigon Orphanage but received very little pay. I was able to help her and her children with their day to day living expenses.

At that time I had a job with ITT/FEC at Tan Son Nhut Air Base working as a secretary and general office clerk for several of the managers. On one occasion I saw one of the managers operating the teletype machine and asked him to teach me that skill. He spent about five minutes with me explaining in general the teletype operation. I was able to learn basic teletype operation very quickly. My salary at ITT/FEC was 35,000 Piaster a month.

I did not receive any support from Bill Wann for almost one year. I was often short of funds. My Vietnamese friends loaned me money when I was in need. I decided to go to see Bill's friend who had lived in the Dalat villa with us but was now working in Saigon. I wanted to find out what was going on with Bill. They promised me that they would contact Bill for me. After a couple of months the friend came to my house in Saigon with food and fruit and told me Bill said he would be sending money to me. In about a month the friend brought me 200 US Dollars from Bill. I was very glad to receive this money. Those 200 US Dollars were the last funds that I ever received from Bill Wann.

ITT/FEC transferred me to the office in downtown Saigon. There I worked as a secretary in the Contracting Office and my salary was raised to 47,000 Piaster a month. They normally provided me a ride home but on some occasions I had to walk. I explained my situation with Bill to my American Manager Supervisor and that I was short of funds. He expressed a desire to help me. There were seven other girls in that office and over 150 Vietnamese working in the ITT/FEC Building.

I was the only one provided transportation. When the others saw that I was being driven in the American vehicles they became jealous and spread rumors that I was fooling around with the Advisors. I had never done anything wrong with any of my bosses in any of the departments of ITT/FEC.

One Saturday afternoon, after work, I went out for a cocktail with the department bosses and they said they would take me home afterwards. I had no idea where we were going. When we walked into a bar it was very dark and we all sat down at the same table. Soon several Vietnamese girls came in and each sat down with one of the men and the men bought the girls drinks. I couldn't believe it. I asked the boss sitting next to me what this was all about. He told me it was a bar to pick up girls. I was very surprised as I had never been to a bar before. I told him I did not like having been taken there. He immediately took me home.

In my office of the Contracting Department there was a large room for teletype communications. One of the girls in that office had problems with her boss. She had been working there for over a year and the boss was not satisfied with her work. The boss met with her and discussed his disappointment with her poor job performance. The next day she called in sick and did not come to work for several days. Her work began to pile up as she was the principle telegraph operator. The boss asked me if I knew how to operate a teletype machine. I told him I had five minutes of training by an operator at Tan Son Nhut Airport, but I thought I could help out for several days until she returned. He spent a few minutes with me to teach me the general requirements. I started working, slow at first, but had no problems getting the work done. I started early in the morning working until almost midnight, by myself. The boss took me home when I completed my work. I worked in that department for three days and nights until midnight. I learned a lot by sending and receiving messages and communicating using the machines in our office. I was able to communicate with operators in Paramus, Hong Kong and the communications center in the United States. I received a very nice letter of appreciation for my work.

When his old clerk returned she saw what I had been doing for him. She was concerned about her job so called the bosses wife and told her he had been working late with me. The wife called me, very mad, cursing me and accusing me of fooling around with her husband. She said that I knew he was married and had two children. I told her the truth about my work and assured her that I was not fooling around with him. She didn't believe me and insisted that I had been having sexual intercourse with her husband. I got very mad and told her husband that he needed to straighten out the matter. I could not continue to take false accusations like that. The next morning I spoke to the senior manager and related what happened. He told me not to worry about it as he would clear it with the husband and wife. Once in a while I would take my children to a party for one of the Advisor's children. My neighbors were always curious when an American would come to pick me up. They would stand by their door and watch disparagingly.

I frequently took my children to the Saigon Market to shop for fruit or enjoy eating a bowl of Pho or noodles at an outside stall. One time a little boy beggar came to us for coins and I decided to get him something to eat rather than money. The Pho shop owner asked me not to do that but I insisted that she give the boy a bowl of soup. The minute the boy sat down up rushed ten more beggars who ran up with their hands out. This time I said no. Sadly, they scooped up and ate the soup left in our bowls.

Our department had to assist other departments, including the publishing department, to catch up on their work. My salary was increased to 57,000 Piaster per month. I kept a little cash for taxi fare and gave the remainder to Mom. I told her to keep the money in a locked drawer. On occasion when Mom would take funds from the drawer she would leave the key out visible to anyone. The money I had given her was gone in two weeks. Mom asked for more but that was all I had. There were eleven people living in our house now and the money could have been taken by anyone. Any item I bought I had to pay for over price. The shops would see that I had American children and demand the very highest prices. On occasion I would bargain down lower than the normal selling price and the seller would curse or spit in front of me.

In January, 1973, the United States signed a Peace Agreement with the North Vietnamese and by March of 1973 all American military units had departed South Vietnam. By the middle of 1973 most of the civilian elements of the United States, such as the US Agency for International Development (USAID), and those of other foreign countries, that had supported the South Vietnamese government, were closing operations. The ITT/FEC terminated me due to a reduction in their force. I was given my full month salary plus sick and annual leave pay when I left. I returned home with a large amount of money which I told Mom to spend carefully as I now didn't have a job.

A month later my older sister referred me to her supervisor, a Catholic Nun, who would assist me in finding a job. The Nun referred me to an American lady who was the Senior Director of FCVN, Friend of Children of Vietnam. Their office was in Denver, Colorado. I immediately applied for a job at their orphanage. I was interviewed by the director, Terry, who hired me as a general office clerk working for 6,000 Piaster a month. This was much less than I was making at ITT/FEC but this was the only opportunity I had to work. The facility had over 200 orphans, from babies to toddlers. Within a month I worked my way up to taking charge of most activities. In addition to the office work of hiring, firing, and payroll I did childcare, nursing and insuring proper nutrition. I also arranged for hospitalization when needed.

Due to my increased responsibilities my salary was raised to 25,000 Piaster a month. I taught the toddlers how to play and have fun. I taught the cooks how to buy and prepare certain foods that would provide good nutrition for the children. I accompanied the chef to the market and showed her the types of vegetables, fruits and meats which were better for the children. I always tasted the food before it was served to the chil-dren. I required all the new employees I hired to attend classes, which I taught, on the specifics of being a Child Care Worker. I taught them how to care for the children from nursing and feeding the babies to personal cleanliness. I issued certificates to them when they completed the training. A sad function of my duties was to care of the burial of the remains of children who died at the orphanage. I would pay the burial man and follow him to the burial site to be sure it was done properly. I quickly found that they were inappropriately burying the bodies in very shallow graves. I had to pay them an additional 500 piaster from my own funds to dig deeper graves. For this I was never repaid.

During this time I would walk to work very early in the morning and not return home until late at night. I did not have much time with my own children and they were continually harassed by their cousins. The twins would cry to me on my return home and tell me what had happened during the day. To get them away from this harassment I decided to send them to a boarding school for American children where they were taught in the Vietnamese and English languages. They remained there for about four months until the Viet Cong increased their attacks and their security became untenable. I continued to search for a way to get my children out of Vietnam.

The manager of the orphanage, Terry, and her assistant Thuy, often went to the Delta area to bring more orphans back to their facility. Thuy saw I was taking charge of everything and became very jealous and looked for ways to discredit me. I usually ate lunch with the orphanage managers and Thuy. That room was next to the room holding the orphanage safe where funds were kept. At her request, I provided Thuy the keys to my desk drawer and the combination to the safe. I trusted her and gave these things to her. One day I placed 5,000 Piaster in my desk drawer to be used to pay the man preparing a grave for a deceased baby. I went to eat lunch. Thuy was not present while we were eating but came in much later. When I finished lunch I went back to get the money and it was gone. I asked Thuy if she had given the money to the grave digger and she replied no. She stated that she had nothing to do with my money. I told the manager that the money was gone and that Thuy was the only one who had access to it besides me. Also the money in the safe was less than recorded. I didn't know who might have taken the money as all the advisors also had the safe combination. This issue was never resolved.

One day the Canadian Catholic Priest, who the Vietnamese called Cha Ngan, brought twelve girls to me and asked me to train them to work at any position available. I accepted all of them and trained them to be child care workers. Later I set up a class for twenty five more girls and also trained them in child care. Of this group of girls, only two initially passed the required testing. I continued to work with them and eventually all were issued Child Care Certificates.

My sister, Lan, worked with Mrs. Nam who had a daughter, Nga, needing work. I hired Nga and taught her to be a child care worker. One day Lan borrowed 4,500 Piasters from Mrs. Nam. Mrs. Nam had her daughter Nga bring the money to me for me to give to my sister. The girl guard opened the gate and saw Nga pass the 4,500 Piaster to me. In a few days Nga had the job. I also hired another friend of Nathan to take care of the Directors children. The guard told the Director that

I was collecting 4,500 Piaster for each of the girls hired, to include those twelve girls brought by Cha Ngan. This was one of several unfortunate incidents which cast false light on my personal behavior.

Almost every day after work I went to look for good powdered milk sold at a reasonable price. One day I took 4,000 Piaster with me to pay for the milk I had ordered the day before. On the way I was stopped by the police who searched my purse. When I visited my Mom at the hospital I found the money was gone. I told my manager, Tom, about it and he did not believe me. Sue, Terry's director, who worked with me daily, believed me. Sue told me to go ahead and get the money needed from the safe. I told her I would repay it when I received my monthly pay.

Terry, the Director's husband, told me that he had heard many rumors about me. He said that the word around was that I was collecting money from the girls I had been training and that I had taken money from the office. I told him I had been telling the truth, that I did not take the money from the safe or desk and that I was not collecting money from the girls. I told him again that all in the office, to include Thuy, Sue, Sue's boyfriend and all Directors had the combination to the safe. Also Thuy had the key to my desk. He offered me one month pay and relieved me of my job. I was so angry I went to the civil court to sue to regain my honesty and trust. The court staff told me I could not win a suit as the others had funds to hire a lawyer for their defense and I had none. They told me to just forget it, which I did.

The next day, Sue, Terry's sister, told me that Terry had a birthday coming up in one week and asked me to stay in my job. I decided to remain and told Sue that I would organize a party with some entertaining to celebrate Terry's birthday. I trained some of the female workers to dance, provide comedy and singing for the party. I did what she asked and the entertainment for the party was well received. I embroidered a dragon on a small tablecloth as a gift to Terry. After a few days I told Sue I was leaving. She asked me not to go but I left, not taking a one month salary which was offered.

I went to my sister's manager, the Nun who had referred me initially for the job. I told her everything that had happened and she believed me. She was pleased that I had trained the 12 girls which Cha Ngan had brought to me. She told me not to worry that she would find me another position. After a conversation with Cha Ngan, she acquired a job for me as a translator at an International Library with a salary of 25,000 Piaster a month. While working for Cha Ngan, he observed that I was always sad and asked me why I was not happy. I told him that I had twins and a family of eleven living in my house and that at times I did not have enough money to buy food for them. I told him that I had been supporting them since 1968.

Cha Ngan helped me write a letter to Bill Wann demanding that he support our children. There was no response to that request. Cha Ngan said he would pray for us all. About a week later Cha Ngan came to my department and asked me not to go home after work that he wanted to talk to me. He said he wanted to talk to an American lady about my personal situation. I waited outside my department for almost two hours. The American lady came out from talking with Cha Ngan and departed without talking to me. He then rushed out and invited me into his office. I was very concerned that I was going to be fired. He handed me a paper bag and said this is for you and your children. I thought it was cookies. He told me that the lady who had just left was the Director of an orphanage whose orphans were gone and the orphanage had closed. The lady gave the priest 47,000 Piaster. Cha Ngan gave me all that money saying that I needed it more than him. He told me he would hold the money for my future use. He asked me how much I needed now. I told him I needed 7,000 Piaster which he immediately gave me. He said he would have his secretary hold the remainder of the funds for my future use. He said I should ask for more when needed for my family. He then told me that I did not have to work for him anymore and that I should stay home and take care of my children during this critical time.

I had my house on the market for sale for almost a year but no one even looked at it. On March 1, 1975, I finally sold my house for 600,000 Piaster. This was 200,000 Piaster below its value but I was glad to get it sold, even at the loss. Before closing we moved to a rental house. My young sister married and moved out. My older sister and her children remained with me but I had to ask her to move even though she had difficulty surviving without my support. I rented a smaller house which I shared with the owner. The owner and his wife stayed upstairs and my Mom, my twins and I lived downstairs.

Following the departure of the American Military the Vietnam War situation was becoming more serious. The attacks by the Communists were more frequent every day. In March of 1975 I told Cha Ngan, that I was worried for the safety of my twins and myself. In the Danang area and other places the Vietnamese-American children were being brutally murdered by the North Vietnamese soldiers. They would torture or decapitate these children in front of their mother or other relatives. Cha Ngan was also concerned and suggested that I give my children to the American orphanage so they would have the opportunity to be sent to the United States. With deep remorse, I agreed to give my children away.

Cha Ngan assisted me in finding an orphanage for my twins. I presented my situation to the first place recommended. I was turned away as they didn't have space for them. I went to a second orphanage and they said I should check back with them in a week. Unfortunately they would not accept my children as all of their orphans had already been processed to leave

Vietnam and that Orphanage was closing. The North Vietnamese forces were speedily approaching Saigon. The Director of that orphanage told me there was not enough time to process my children for evacuation. When I told Cha Ngan of my situation, he told me of an orphanage nearby and that I should check with them. That place was Vietnamese American Children's Fund (V.A.C.F.) orphanage located at 27 Ky Dong Street, Saigon. Cha Ngan convinced their director, Victor Srinivasan to accept my children.

I explained to Mr. Srinivasan my grief for giving up my children but that I hoped for a better life for them if they could get to America. It was very painful to sign the necessary papers to give my children away. He explained that he would help to find a good American family to adopt my children. My children were placed in the V.A.C.F orphanage. I was seriously grieved by taking this action. Daniel and Cathy were just five years old.

I carefully packed their favorite clothes in a small suitcase and prepared them to go to the orphanage. They asked, "Where are we going?" I told them that they were going to America with the other children to get away from the war. They really didn't understand what I was talking about. They both cried profusely as they didn't want to go by themselves. I explained to them that they would have to stay in the orphanage for a few days and wait for a flight to America to see their daddy. They asked me if I would be going with them and I responded, "Yes".

During this time the North Vietnamese Army continued to rapidly advance south. They had taken control of Ban Me Thuot in the Central Highlands and were about to overrun Danang. The roads were crowded with people in cars, buses and walking, with all of their belongings, rushing south.

On March 18, 1975, I took my twins to the V.A.C.F. orphanage. Again they sadly cried. They didn't like their new home. They fought with the other children and workers there. They would often stand by the gate hoping that I would appear. My Mom and I both cried. Mom was very mad with me and said I had foolishly given my children away. I kept telling her that it was for their safety rather than seeing them chopped to pieces as the North Vietnamese Army soldiers had done to Vietnamese-American children in Hue and Danang. Further, having worked for the Americans, I was on the Communist list to be killed and if I were caught the children would also be killed.

For several nights I could not sleep. I was missing my children and very worried about the current status of the Communist taking over the country. During the night, when I was half asleep, I saw a vision of myself walking the red carpet again. Beside me were guardian angels, ladies, gentlemen and youngsters. They kneeled down as I walked by. I walked toward the image of God and cried. I asked why I must give my children away. God answered, "It's not for just you my child but it is for all in need. Do not be sad but believe in me. I will make things happen. The children will be safe and you will go to America with them". I told this story to my Mom and she said it was just a dream. She told me that I should not believe that I would be able to accompany my children to America. At this time I felt that I was a very true servant of god.

About a week later, Mr. Sarinivasan told me that he could not get an American foster parent for my twins but that he had New Zealand foster parents for them. I did not want them to go to New Zealand. I asked if he could find foster parents from England or Australia. I told him that I would like to talk to any prospective parent before signing any papers for adoption. He told me that the war situation was so grave that he was very concerned about getting all of the orphanage children out of the country as soon as possible. I asked him if there was any way I could go to America with my children. He responded, "Not at this time". I felt very sad after hearing this but I continued to have hope. In late March I took my twins from the orphanage to eat and to shop for some clothes. I returned to the orphanage about 4 in the afternoon. Cathy was wearing a paper crown I bought at the market.

When we arrived at the orphanage there was an ABC News correspondent waiting to talk to me. He asked if I could speak English and asked if he could interview me about my feelings on the current war situation. He asked if he could help. I did not have time to get permission from the Director to talk to the press but I went ahead and talked to him. The reporter made a video of me and the children. I told him that due to the seriousness of the war situation I had decided to give my children away for their safety. As I had been working for the Americans my children and I were destined to be murdered by the Communist if they would overrun the country. I wanted them to have a full life in America. I told the reporter that I had tried with three different orphanages but none would accept them for adoption. I told him I wanted them to go to America and I wanted to go with them. He took our picture and recorded my story. This interview was telecast on

ABC News, throughout the United States on Saturday, April 5, 1975.

At this time hundreds of Vietnamese families who had worked for the Americans and American civilians who had been working in Vietnam were being bused to Tan San Nhut Airport, loaded on large U.S. Air Force jets and flown out of the country. On April 4, 1975, at 4:45 PM, a large U.S Air Force C-5A airplane crashed due to a mechanical problem. This plane was loaded with 328 passengers, which included Vietnamese-American orphans, accompanying adults, Defense Attache officers and crew. 78 children died in the crash. Also dead were 31 accompanying adults, 35 Defense Attache officers and 11 crew members. There were only 173 survivors. At the time of the crash the North Vietnamese Army had taken over the outskirts of Saigon.

Meanwhile I continued to go to the United States Embassy trying to get the required authorization to get my twins and me out of the country. There were hundreds of people rushing the fence trying to get the necessary visas to leave Vietnam. Due to the crowds I wasn't even able to get close to the gate. I went home feeling terrible and did not know what to do. I told Mr. Srivarasan, the V.A.C.F. Director, my dilemma and he said he knew the Embassy would be difficult. He told me that all of the American orphanages had already left country and he was trying to get another Exit Visa for an airplane to take the children that remained in V.A.C.F.

Not known to me at this time were the activities of a group of Americans, with prior activities in Vietnam, who were doing everything possible to get the Vietnamese-American children, who had been left behind, out of the country. They had heard that the South Vietnamese government was allowing these children to leave the country but the United States government was not cooperating. They were writing letters and sending telegrams to their legislators and foreign officials, specifically for my family they had seen on the ABC News special, to grant visas for us to leave the country. Also, there was a group of Chamber of Commerce Members in Anchorage, Alaska that had raised $130,000.00 in small donations who were arranging for an aircraft to fly to Saigon and pick up the children from the V.A.C.F.

On April 12, 1975, Mr. Srivarasan, sent a worker to my home with a message that he wanted to see me the next day. The next day on my visit with the Director, he gave me sponsorship papers he had received from Mr. Raymond C. Kirtland offering to sponsor my children and me to America.

Mr. Kirtland, in 1966 and 1967, had taught English at the Vietnamese American Association School in Saigon. I was surprised, shocked and shaking all over having received these sponsorship papers and immediately agreed to this action. I did not know that Mr. Kirtland, unknown to me, had viewed Cathy, Daniel and me on the ABC news segment, April 5, 1975. He had been deeply moved by our situation to the point he could not sleep. He contacted his State Assemblymen and Congressmen and even high ranking Vietnamese, he had previously known in Vietnam, in an attempt to obtain exit visas, not only for me and my twins but for the remaining orphans at the V.A.C.F.

On April 13, 1975 I went to see the Director and he told me that Mr. Kirtland wants to bring my children and me to America but he does not know yet how to get us out of country. Approximately one half hour later several ladies from the American Embassy came to the orphanage and we had a meeting in the upstairs office with Mrs. Srivarasan. She introduced me to American Embassy ladies telling them that I also needed help to get out of Vietnam. They were very concerned about how to get an airplane to get the children out. At the same time, I was notified that Mr. Kirtland had called the Director and expressed concern about my children and me. Mr. Kirtland told the Director that funds had been raised for transportation of the remainder of the orphanage children and that there was an aircraft standing by for us.

For the next two days I continued to try to get into the American Embassy compound to obtain exit visas but again because of the crowds I could not even get near the gate. There were thousands of people pushing and fighting to get through the gate. They were even trying to climb the walls. The American military police were using extreme force to keep them back and protect the gates. I remained, pushing with the crowd.

The North Vietnamese Army was rapidly closing in on all areas around Saigon. Thousands of refugees from the Northern Provinces were crowding Saigon streets. Time passed very slowly and I was trying to get my house sold. On April 22, 1975, I finally received clearance from the Vietnamese Land Management office to sell my house and transfer the title to the new owner. I was told to pay a fee of 20,000 Piaster and the person in charge told me I would have to wait a week for the paperwork. I begged him to get the papers available right away as I was leaving country. He told me he had to wait for more signatures. When I asked if there was any way to speed up the action he asked to talk to me outside. Outside he told me that if I would give him 5,000 Piaster he needed to bribe others, he could get the papers right away. I gave him the requested money and waited outside his office for about one half hour. He then came out and handed me the paperwork which was the title of my house for the new owner.

The new owner brought me a basket full of Piaster. I had the money but continued to have a difficult time trying all possible avenues to get out of Vietnam with my children. On April 23, 1975, I received a telegram from Mr. Raymond Kirtland which stated that my children and I are related to him. It was written that I am his fiancée. I took all my papers and this telegram to the American Embassy but again could not get to the gate. As during days before, thousands of people crowded around the Embassy walls. Again some were trying to climb over the wall or slip through the fences. I was one of several hundred people standing by the main gate area, pushing and shoving to get ahead and through the main gate. They were letting a few people in at a time. The guards were having a difficult time keeping the crowd from forcing the gate open. I stayed there until after dark and then returned home. I did the same thing for the next three days.

On the fourth day as I was standing by the gate at about noon time, a bus came by and announced that anyone married to an American, with the proper paperwork, to present their papers. They would then take these persons inside for processing. Even though I didn't have marriage papers the officer saw the papers I had and let me on the bus. Inside the gate there was the same problem of many people in line waiting to be processed. I waited there until that office closed and had to return home. It was announced that everyone had to present original marriage papers, which I did not have. Regardless, I remained in the line until the office closed and then returned home.

I eventually went out through the back gate where I saw a man with a child approach an American Military Policeman with a paper bag full of money. He asked the American to take the money and to get his child out of Vietnam. The guard, very properly, would not do anything for the man. As I passed the guard I told him about my situation. He told me that often families would come with large sums of money and even gold to get help getting out of the country. The guard allowed me to pass and return home.

I arrived home, again feeling very sad. My Mom got upset with me again and demanded that I go to the orphanage and bring the children home. I remained calm and firm in my decision to get my children to safety. I told my Mom that I would keep trying to get Daniel and Cathy out of Vietnam, even until the last day before the Communist would occupy Saigon. Only then would I bring them home. All I could do now was pray and believe what God had told me, "That he would take care, that I would not lose my children".

On the afternoon of April 27, 1975, a worker from the V.A.C.F. orphanage came to my house and told me I must see Mr. Srivirasani right away. I rushed to see him and he told me that I must pack my things and be prepared to depart for the United States the next day. I would be limited to take one small suitcase and a carryon bag for each person. I was shocked and happy. I couldn't believe that my wishes to be with my children had come true. What God had told me had become a reality. The actions of Mr. Kirtland identified him as a God fearing man and that he had been chosen by God to be the personal benefactor of me and my children.

I gave 350,000 Piaster to my sister Lan to buy the house she was renting and to build a second floor as a place for Mom to live. I told her that when I leave she should bring Mom to her house and take care of her. I gave Mom the remainder of my money, gold and diamonds and left with the hope that Mom would settle in with my sister. My brother, Nathan, gave me a few dollars and said goodbye. Later, when in America, I learned that Lan mistreated Mom and wanted her to leave the house. Lan also did not want my young sister to stay even one night. The situation was so bad that Mom had to work hard and save money to rent a small apartment for herself in a neighbor's house. My brother, Nathan, at that time was having problems with his wife, so he also stayed for a while with Mom in her small apartment.

On the afternoon of April 28, 1975, Cathy, Daniel and I boarded a bus with the other orphanage children. Each worker carried a small child. We arrived at the Tan Son Nhut Airport gate around 3 P.M. After being checked by the Vietnamese Police and the American Military Police we were driven to a Caribou type aircraft that had been hired by the Alaska Chamber of Commerce. The airport runways had been damaged so badly by North Vietnamese Army rockets that the larger jet aircraft were no longer able to take off and land. Our smaller plane was able to take off at 5:30 that evening. This was the last fixed wing aircraft to leave Tan Son Nhut Airport before the Communist forces took over. As we departed the Communist began heavy bombardment of the airfield. All later evacuation from the Saigon area had to be by Helicopter, either from a guarded helipad on the Embassy grounds or from rooftops. These helicopters were flying back and forth to neighboring countries or to boats in the South

China Sea. On April 30, 1975, the North Vietnamese Communist had taken over Saigon and control of all of South Vietnam. Saigon was renamed Ho Chi Minh City.

In the early morning of April 29, 1975, we arrived at Clark Airbase in the Philippine Islands. The children were kept in a separate area away from the adults. A child care worker provided night clothes for the children to sleep. She took all of their clothes to wash and the next morning mixed up the clothes she issued to each child. Cathy and Daniel could not find their favorite clothes, those they had worn to the Tan Son Nhut Airport. They were upset because they had lost their best clothes during that time they were with the other orphanage children. I stayed with the other refugee adults in a tent and slept on a folding cot. In the morning of the next day I contacted Mr. Raymond Kirtland to let him know that we were out of Vietnam. After a few days I had my children with me and we remained together at the military base. A week later we were flown to the United States Territory island of Guam. During that trip I lost my bag with all my important papers and pictures. On Guam we all stayed in a refugee camp, six persons to a tent.

At the Guam refugee camp I met Terry, the FCVN (Friend of Children of Vietnam) orphanage Senior Director, whom I had worked for in Vietnam. While in Saigon I had gone to her for help to get my children to America and she had refused to assist me. She was shocked and personally ashamed when she saw me on Guam. I also met Bill Wann's friend who was glad to see we had gotten out of Vietnam. There on Guam I met a personal friend who was with me at Convent Des Oiseaux School. She had gone to Project Concern in Dampao, Lam Dong, Dalat with me and we had seen doctors there. When on Guam I gave her my warm jacket and she gave me three Vietnamese style dresses, Ao Dais.

We remained in the Guam Refugee Camp for about two weeks and then were flown to Fort Chaffee, Arkansas, where we were kept while our immigration papers were being processed. Mr. Kirtland sent me fifty dollars and pictures while at Fort Chaffee. On May 31, 1975, Cathy, Daniel and I departed Fort Chaffee, flying to Oklahoma City by Frontier Airlines, then to Los Angeles by American Airlines and finally on to Santa Barbara on United Airlines. It was an interesting experience for one who had never travelled before to negotiate different airports and changing airlines.

We finally arrived in Santa Barbara, California at 9:40 PM on May 31, 1975. On arrival in Santa Barbara, I wore one Ao Dais, which had been given by my friend. That initial meeting was very exciting. Mr. Kirtland met us at the runway with news people as soon as the plane stopped. They took our picture which was on the front page of the Santa Barbara News the next day. We were identified as Vietnamese Refugees sponsored by Mr. Raymond Kirtland and the Montecito Presbyterian Church.

Each day during these past months of turmoil, the children and I could have been killed by the North Vietnamese or their Vietcong supporters. Thanks mainly to the attention and assistance provided by

SANTA BARBARA NEWS-PRESS

B SECTION   SANTA BARBARA, CALIFORNIA, MONDAY EVENING, JUNE 2, 1975   C   PAGE B-1

Refugee mother, twins arrive in Santa Barbara

A seemingly impossible morass of red tape and confusion has ended happily in Santa Barbara for a Vietnamese mother and her 6-year-old half-American twins.

Tuyet Mai Lam and the twins, Cathy and Daniel, arrived at the Santa Barbara Airport late Saturday night, a month and a half after their plight in Vietnam was noticed and acted upon by Raymond Kirtland of 6565 Sabado Tarde, Isla Vista, helped by El Montecito Presbyterian Church.

"Theirs was the very last plane load of orphans and refugees to get out of Vietnam," Kirtland said.

THE LITTLE FAMILY came to Kirtland's attention while he viewed an ABC-TV newscast in early April. The family, according to the newscast, was destined to be split up permanently when the mother placed Cathy and Daniel with the Vietnamese American Children's Fund Orphanage in Saigon.

The reason for placement in the orphanage, Kirtland said, was that Mrs. Lam felt the children would have a better chance of survival with an American family.

But happily, Kirtland said, the mother was allowed to accompany the children out of Saigon as a chaperone.

"The family will literally take over my apartment," Kirtland said. "I'm moving out for a while."

KIRTLAND and the church acted as co-sponsors for the family, and managed to fight their way through "red tape you wouldn't believe," according to Kirtland, which included the official sanctioning of the orphanage by the South Vietnamese government.

The church women's association is organizing a shower for the family, Kirtland said. Persons with items to donate may call 968-0090 or 963-8621.

Mr. Victor Srinivasan, Director of the Vietnamese American Children's Fund Orphanage, the Alaskan Chamber of Commerce and Mr. Raymond C. Kirtland, we live today. My tale of my efforts to leave Vietnam with my Vietnamese-American children resembled the intensity of any spy thriller, complicated by a bout with American bureaucracy. This phase of my adventure finally ended when my children and I arrived at the Santa Barbara airport.

Daniel and Cathy are now enjoying a healthy, happy lifestyle, with the responsibly of caring for children of their own.

SUZANNE

When I came to the United States of America, for convenience in conversation, I adopted the Anglicized name of Suzanne. On arrival in Santa Barbara Mr. Raymond Kirtland had prepared living space for Cathy, Daniel and me in his personal apartment. He moved to separate accommodations for himself. We first talked for hours, getting to know each other. We shared our experiences from the many actions just to get out of Vietnam, through the refugee camps and the travel in the United States.

Raymond's first personal assistance to me was to bandage my feet. He had seen me walking with a limp as we got off the airplane. I had blisters from walking in tight, new shoes. In order to learn of our new surroundings, Raymond, without delay, taught me how to use the household appliances, all unfamiliar to me. It was exciting to learn the special qualities of the stove, the dishwasher, the garbage disposal and the clothes washing machine and dryer. It was a thrill to learn this modern way of living in the United States. I was accustomed to washing clothes by hand and hanging them on an outside line to dry. I had cooked on metal racks over burning wood or charcoal in hard clay stoves.

Raymond took us for a drive around Santa Barbara. I was amazed by the bright wide streets filled with fast moving fancy cars, trucks and busses. Quite a difference from Saigon's narrow crowded streets filled with bicycles, families on Cyclos, many walkers and venders on the sidewalks selling their goods. It had been common on the Saigon streets to see farmers walking down the middle of the street with their goods balanced on the ends of a long pole over their shoulder, on the way to market. Our new home in Santa Barbara was an immediate, exciting experience. Raymond assisted me in improving my English through our conversations and his encouragement for me to carefully watch and listen to television programs. One of my best tutors was "Sesame Street". I was very surprised and embarrassed to see TV programs advertising clothing items such as bras and panties and personal feminine products.

After a short period both Cathy and Daniel were found to be Tuberculosis positive and required to be hospitalized for three weeks followed by medication for the next two years. My tests were negative but because I had just come from Vietnam I was required to take the tubercular medication for a year. After the twins were released from the hospital Raymond took us to the Montecito Presbyterian Church to meet the people who had co-sponsored our escape from Vietnam. They were very happy to have been able to help us and continued to assist with funds for clothing for the children. Raymond arranged for Cathy and Daniel to attend nursery school. With the background of some

English learned at the American school in Vietnam, they quickly learned to talk with their classmates.

While the children were going to school, I asked Raymond's sister, who was a medical doctor, to assist me in finding work. She took me to the University of Santa Barbara to make application for a job. I had a very difficult time completing their long, detailed application form. Not having all of my records, it was very difficult recalling previous jobs, dates, and times. I spent over an hour completing the forms. Raymond's sister was not impressed with my performance and when we returned home she related that to Raymond. She stated that I appeared not to be very smart and was a potential loser. She felt that I would be a burden to him. I heard her arguments but did not reply. She made none of these comments to me and it was not an appropriate time for me to prove my worth.

During this time the only personal clothes I had were those brought from Vietnam. Raymond took me shopping for a new wardrobe at the Ventura Mall. The ladies dresses available were all too large for me, even the size 5 for petites did not fit. I decided to buy material and sew my own dresses. I made my own patterns and sewed by hand dresses that fit very well. Later, Raymond would buy me a sewing machine. Learning to use the machine was an interesting exercise. I kept doing something wrong which caused the thread to keep breaking or getting tangled. With the help of Raymond's mother I learned how to properly thread the bobbin. This had been my major problem and when corrected all sewing went smoothly.

A very nice lady, Mrs. Pearl Cubeca from the First Baptist Church, came to our apartment with many very nice clothes for me and the children. She had seen the news stories of our arrival and had personally collected items for us. She also assisted greatly by taking me around the area while Raymond was at work. During these early days, since my Vietnamese-English vocabulary was much better than most of the refugees, I spent many hours assisting other refugees in translating English language actions and documents. I would frequently accompany them to medical appointments or just grocery shopping, all to assist their integration into their new United States surroundings.

After over six months of trying I became very disappointed at not finding a job. We moved from the Goleta apartment to a house in San Vicente. During this time Raymond assisted another refugee family. A young Vietnamese lady, Huong, with her baby and husband, were sponsored by a lady who gave them a very difficult time. The sponsor required them to work outside in the hot sun and Huong frequently would be sick from overwork. The tough work also generated arguments within the refugee couple. The arguments became so intense that the sponsor lady did not want Huong and the baby living in her house. Raymond took Huong and her baby to live briefly with us. The husband remained with the sponsor. In a short while the husband found a job and a home for the family to live together.

On one of my outings with Mrs. Cubeca she asked if I would like to apply for a job at the Bank of America. Of course I said yes but knew I had no banking experience and would have to learn quickly. I had never even had a checking account as all transactions in Vietnam were in cash. Mrs. Cubeca took me to the bank to make application and to take their required tests. I did not complete the required test in time allotted and came home very sad thinking I would not pass. Within fifteen minutes of arriving home I received a call from the bank saying that I had passed the tests with high scores and they would hire me as a bookkeeper. I went to work for the Santa Barbara Bank of America the next day.

During the next few months I quickly learned many details of banking operations. I learned the operation of the Bank NCR computer which in those days was a large frame of electronic equipment with many operating keys. I had to sit on a high chair to reach and rapidly punch the keys. I was not able to function as fast as I should so my supervisor recommended that I work as a Teller. One of my side functions was to respond to customers requests for status of their accounts. In those years that information was not available automatically. I very strictly followed the bank procedures for identification of customers before providing their bank status. I always would go through the many personal questions the bank required for identification. Unfortunately several of the long time customers of the bank did not like my questioning and complained to my management. Management chastised me and I was very briskly told that I should recognize the bank's long time customers and provide them their requested data without a lot of questions. After a short time, due to the difficulties I had in adjusting to my new and differing job requirements, my manager terminated my services.

With the help of Raymond and a friend, Gilbert Simpson, who knew me and Bill Wann in Vietnam, I contacted Bill. With the assistance of the Attorney General of Santa Barbara, the Santa Barbara Court directed child support for Cathy and Daniel. Bill came to Santa Barbara and took us to a U.S. military facility to obtain identification cards for me and the children. This was to provide authorization to use military medical facilities and the military exchanges. Cathy and Daniel did not know their father so I identified him as a friend of Raymond who they identified as their father. I waited until they were nine years old before telling the twins the identity of their true father.

Raymond decided to teach me how to drive so I would not have to depend on him to get me to work. After a few efforts Raymond became so nervous with me driving he turned the job over to our friend Sherry. Sherry was a good instructor and I very soon received my license. Now as a licensed driver Raymond gave me his Honda Civic to drive myself to work. Raymond demonstrated much love and concern for me and the children while he was our sponsor. During this time Raymond was hired as a Property Manager for a large firm in Tennessee and was required to relocate.

After having acted as our sponsor for a year Raymond found us a place to live in the cottage of Mrs. Ester Paglioti there in El Montecito. Ester was a dear lady who showed much love and care for the children. She would watch them while I was at work, take them to school, wash their clothes, feed them and make sure they bathed properly. She treated me as her own daughter and the twins as grandchildren.

After a few months Raymond returned to Ester's house in El Montecito and asked me to marry him. I was very pleased to say yes. Ester organized a delightful engagement party for our friends at her cottage. We were married on August 14, 1976 at the El Montecito Presbyterian Church in Santa Barbara,

California. The wedding ceremony was wonderful. I wore a Western style wedding dress and later the Ao Dai, the Vietnamese style dress. Many church friends and members of Raymond's family attended. Many of my Vietnamese relatives and friends were also there. I was very pleased that they included a group of ladies, who were also mothers of twins, were also present. I learned that they frequently met together and asked me to join their group. Ester hosted the entire festivities. Following that delightful day, Ester took care of the twins while Raymond and I went on a honeymoon.

We moved to a large house in the Concord section of San Francisco. Raymond drove a U-Haul with all of our goods and I drove the Honda with the children. In San Francisco I was able to get a job as teller at a Wells Fargo Bank. After a few weeks I found that the drive was too long and resigned the position.

One weekend Raymond drove me and the children to Mantica, California in an effort to visit Bill Wann. When we arrived at his home I saw him in his yard. Raymond called to Bill and asked him to meet with us in a nearby McDonald's restaurant or anywhere else he may wish to go. Bill Wann refused to see us.

Raymond found work in San Francisco. He would drive the Honda to work. That left me driving the large truck. I had found a job as teller with the New Chartered Bank of London. They first sent me for training in their San Francisco facility. I would take the Bark under the Bay for the instruction. On one occasion traffic stopped for over an hour under the water. Everyone was in a panic. I was not really sure what was going on. Fortunately, all cleared and we were on our way. After two weeks of training in San Francisco with other members of the

New Charter Bank staff, I began to work as a Teller in Concord. My work went very smoothly and I had no problems with my accounts.

One day a customer came to my position to change money. He was changing small bills to large bills and some larger bills to smaller ones. As he left my position I realized that he had tricked me in the exchanges. I ran out of the bank to catch him but he had disappeared. I immediately reported the incident to my supervisor and indicated that I might be short funds due to the trickery. Surely at the end of the day I was short $200.00. The next day the bank manager called me into his office for me to explain my shortage. I told him that I had reported the incident to my supervisor and that I had tried to catch the perpetrator. We learned that the trickster was not a regular bank customer and had left no trace as who he might be. As a new employee I did not think fast enough to push the emergency alarm button which would have immediately closed the entry doors and probably caught the thief.

On one occasion the door to my little safe snapped shut and smashed my thumb which ended swollen and black and blue. I ended up losing my nail from that incident. At the end of work one day, when preparing to go home I could not start my truck. I called home for Raymond to come and assist me. My manager saw me having problems and came to help. He was able to start the truck immediately. He told me that all I had to do was turn the locked steering wheel. When Raymond arrived the truck started with no problem.

Raymond bought me some very nice clothes for work and I also made many things for myself. One day a co-worker liked the jump suit I was wearing and asked where I had bought it. She was very surprised when I told her I had made it myself. She liked the way it was designed and how well it fitted and asked if I could make one for her daughter. I told her I was sorry but that I only made clothes for myself. She then asked for my pattern and I told her I did not use a pattern but just measured and cut and that I had not had formal training as a seamstress. She passed this word to all of our fellow employees who also praised my very special clothes.

After a while we moved to another apartment. Raymond left us for about a month, going to Indiana to do a remodeling job for his father. He remodeled a grocery store into an office complex. At our new apartment we met another Vietnamese lady who had married and American. Quite often we were invited to her home to eat Vietnamese food. One evening she asked if I had adequate spending money for myself and my children. When I told her we lived day to day she said I should come to work with her in San Francisco where she made a lot of tips. I told her that I did not want to leave my children alone at home at night.

During this time I attended college at night to study English. After completing his work for his father Raymond returned to Concord and moved us to Indiana. We had an apartment in the basement of his father's house. I was able to get a job as Customer Representative and Auditor for the National Bank of Crown Point. The pay was not as good as I wanted but the position was exciting and carried a lot of responsibility. Due to the heavy work load I routinely was the last one to leave the office at night. I had to wait for the daily reports from the branch managers and on occasion reports from supervisors of eight branches. I was required to assure that each report was correct and to call the preparer if there was an error. I then was required to submit our daily report to our Oakland office. This report included checking and savings, time deposits, cashier's checks, money orders, traveler's checks, federal deposits, all types of bonds and other transactions. Monthly I was required to count and balance all Travelers Checks, the cash in our vault and cash actions by our teller supervisors.

On several occasions I was chastised for providing information to customers that was in error or for an action that was not completed correctly. I found that my assistant was not following my instructions and was offering customers bad advice. When she had an action which she was not familiar with she was required to refer the customer to me. Also any report submitted from my office required my review before being forwarded. This was not always done. Several times a customer would go direct to my assistant rather than consulting me. It was very obvious that the customer did not want to deal with an Asian. I was deeply insulted by this prejudice but did not let it affect my job performance.

After a while, with the help of Raymond's parents for a down payment, we bought a house in Lake-of-Four-Seasons, Indiana. This was a very nice new house which we bought for under $50,000.00. The weather in Indiana in the winter can be very cold. When at work, looking out the window, I saw snowflakes for the first time. I remarked to my co-worker how beautiful it was and how much I liked it. She replied to me, "Just wait and see if you like it when you have been in it for a while". In just a few weeks the weather began getting colder and the snow heavier. I had to wear layers of warm clothes to just go outside and when going to work to keep warm. After a few weeks the snow began to come more frequently and heavier. On a few occasions the snow was so high that it was difficult to open the front door. Some days the temperature would go below zero degrees and freeze the house water pipes. It also made it difficult to start the car and many co-workers could not get to work. More than three times a year the snow was so heavy that offices, banks and schools were closed. The children loved to play in the snow in the front yard and make snow men. The nearby lake was frozen over.

After the snow melted there was still ice on the roadway. When driving home one afternoon I had to stop quickly. The car spun around and luckily I did not hit anyone or do any damage but I was very scared. After that incident Raymond gave me a very helpful lesson on how to apply brakes without losing traction. One evening, for a special treat, Raymond took the children and me to see the Star Wars first special edition of the movie. When we arrived at the theater we found all the tickets had been sold. After waiting we were able to get two seats on the front row for Cathy and Daniel. Raymond and I went home and returned for the children after the show.

Raymond was very anxious for me and the children to see and experience many different things in our new American surroundings. He took us site seeing on most every weekend. We would go shopping in the Malls and eat at special places. He took us to a restaurant quite far away to have Vietnamese food. On one occasion he wanted us to see a play, the Nutcracker, playing in

Chicago. He picked me up from work for me to change, get the children and make the long, heavily trafficked drive to the theater. We were late arriving at the theater, the show was almost over and we had to stand by the last row to see what remained of the show. I felt very bad for Raymond who had wanted us to have a special treat. Raymond's special efforts for us were much more costly than he could afford.

The marriage between Raymond and me was not harmonious. Cathy and Daniel went to Indiana Public School in the Elementary grades. Raymond was very controlling with everything I did. I frequently experienced his demanding little actions like publicly correcting me in front of others. This was very embarrassing for me but it meant little to him. I found it more and more difficult to talk to him and to share personal feelings.

I was not comfortable being under the constant strict control and direction by my husband. I wanted a sharing relationship and equal rights. I did appreciate that Raymond was a good man, bringing me and my children to the United States and providing a father for my children. I was immature then, had a personal lack of patience but felt that I did not want to live with Raymond anymore. I started making plans to leave Raymond. I told Raymond that I wanted a divorce.

When I told my co-workers at the bank I was planning a divorce they wouldn't believe it. From the outside everything looked as we were a loving couple. When I told my personnel boss she was shocked. The first thing she asked was "what is your share?" When I told her "nothing" she offered to get me a lawyer to be paid for by the bank. Unfortunately the marriage ended in 1978. Raymond asked me to sign off on the house, the furnishings and everything related. Raymond told me that I could have the house if I paid the mortgage. At that time I had no money and could see no way to pay the mortgage so I signed off everything.

I discussed my problem with my friend, Mrs. Simpson who introduced me by phone to her sister in Hawaii. Her sister related that she could find me a job at the restaurant where she worked in Hawaii. At my request, Raymond bought me an airline ticket to Hawaii and he agreed to take care of the children until I could get situated there. Raymond's mother offered me money but I refused.

In late 1978, I flew to Hawaii with only $142.00 in my pocket to begin my life as a single woman with two children. I was able to stay with a Vietnamese friend for a short while. After three weeks I had Raymond send my children to me. He paid their airfare to join me.

My friend convinced me to work in the restaurant where she worked. When I accompanied her to work I was surprised as the surroundings appeared more like a bar than a restaurant, which I was expecting. My friend introduced me to her supervisor called "Mama". I thought this was her real name but later learned that she was called that as she was the one who acted as the "Mother Hen" to all the women working there. I was accepted immediately to work. After a few hours many more women came to work and soon men started to arrive. There was no question that this was a bar. It was very obvious that the men were there for sexual gratification and the women were doing anything necessary with their bodies to sell drinks and make tips. I remained in a corner feeling very uncomfortable. Mama came to me and took me to a table to sit with a group of men. I did not let anyone touch my body so did not make the tips the other women were making. I even had one customer tell me that I didn't belong there. I remained there for eight days, only because I had no other work, and then resigned.

With my banking experience, I found work at the Hawaiian Bank. The pay was not enough to cover my expenses. My formal education and business experiences in Vietnam had placed me well ahead of those with an advanced college degree. I felt it necessary to continue my academic studies to adapt my Asian expertise to the Anglican way of doing things. I decided to study Business Administration and Accounting in a local college. My friend Anh Thuy helped me by taking care of my children while I was at work and in school. After school hours I worked in the Administrative Office of the college. I also worked part time at the Governor's office and as a waitress in a proper evening restaurant. I was rarely home before eleven at night and the children were usually asleep. Even with three jobs I did not have enough income to pay my portion of the rent and other expenses. Again, as I had done on my arrival in California, I assisted newly arriving Vietnamese refugees with learning the English language, completing required documentation and even assisting in obtaining drivers licenses.

To supplement my income, I decided to add Real Estate Sales to my curriculum. My college counselor advised against this. She said my limited knowledge of the English language would make it too difficult for me to learn. I sought the advice of the Real Estate instructor and she encouraged me to take the course. I added Real Estate to my curriculum and was one of 3 out of 27 students to pass the State test. I showed my Real Estate teacher these results and she was surprised but pleased for me. I was able to use Real Estate Sales for limited added income.

My friend suggested that I apply for Social Welfare assistance but I refused. I did not want to live under government support. After a few weeks my friend kept insisting that I at least apply to Social Welfare for assistance in getting an apartment. I went to the Social Welfare Office with her to find what they could do to assist me. After completing the necessary paperwork, to include my divorce papers, I was told I would have to report my employment status weekly. I was concerned how I would have the time to make those weekly reports while working three jobs and going to school. After a few weeks I was notified by the Social Worker of an apartment available for me. I was very excited about this but found when I contacted the renter they would not accept the deduction required by a welfare payment. A month later I was contacted again that welfare had an apartment for me and the children. All I had to do was meet the manager, sign the necessary paperwork and move in.

After completing the formalities we moved into this apartment and remained for a year with Social Welfare paying the rent. During this time the apartment manager continued to become more personally friendly with me and after a short time he made unsolicited sexual advances. I refused any contact with him. This obviously upset him and when my year of free rent ended he told me that he had increased the rent requirement by $10.00. He said that Social Welfare would not accept the increase and that I would have to move. I told him I would pay the $10.00 rent increase. He refused and said that I would have to pay the entire rent myself or move out. Since the only support I had was from Social Welfare, I found another apartment and paid from my own funds.

Daniel continued to be sick due to tonsillitis. After a Doctor removed his tonsils his sickness declined. Daniel began to develop a difficult attitude and was not doing well in school. His doctor advised me that his problem was primarily due to lack of personal care from me. He said that I must have more time with my children. Raymond came to Hawaii twice to visit us and provided funds to send Cathy to a private Catholic school. Also he paid for Cathy and Daniel to participate in a gymnastic program. This continued for a year until I became uncomfortable for him to spend money on the children and asked him to stop the support.

During his second visit, I had started dating Mr. Lance Taniyama, who I eventually married. Lance was a Major in the U.S. Army Reserve and our relationship initially was very good. I soon found that after selling his condominium he spent all of his funds gambling and on other women. He could not keep a decent job and spent many nights out with his friends. His parents did not like me as they thought I was spending all of his money. The situation soon became untenable and I threw his clothes out of our quarters and chased him away. Unfortunately this did not change his behavior.

I also had a job as an office clerk with a private company. That work was well below my capabilities but it was not difficult and the pay was good. In that job I quickly found that the bookkeeper was not very smart and mistakes by her were always blamed on someone else. The Owner and the Manager also did inventory on occasion and frequently made mistakes themselves. When the mistakes were discovered they were always blamed on me. One day after being accused several times by the owner of doing wrong I proved that I had not made a mistake, and that the bookkeeper, the manager or even the owner himself, were in error. The other employees were surprised that I would dare to bring this to the attention of the owner. I spent some thirty minutes arguing my case but was denied. I quit the job.

Fortunately during this time I had interviewed for a position as office manager and controller for an island taxi/tour company and was accepted. I started to work the next day. I learned that the company was operating 143 taxis all over the island of Oahu. To my surprise I found the company was deeply in debt to the Internal Revenue Service. In coordination with the company's legal staff, I quickly developed procedures to deal with the tax problem. In a very short time I was able to clear this tax problem which had plagued the company for years. After one year in this job I assisted in the increase of the number of taxis to 602. The owner was an older lady who was very pleased with my work and was very generous with me. A daughter of the older lady became very jealous of the attention given to me by her mother and took a number of actions against me which made the job untenable. After three years I resigned the position.

I found a job with a distribution firm which provided good pay and benefits. That job only lasted two months as I refused to tolerate sexual harassment by the owner. Every time he would enter my office he would fondle my breasts and other body parts. I informed the person hired to replace me of his unacceptable attention.

I decided to establish a business and go to work for myself. I borrowed funds from a bank to open a small store selling groceries and alcoholic beverages. I also set up a fast food counter in the Oahu International Market. Very soon these businesses proved to be non-productive, not because of mismanagement but due to uncontrollable, repeated thefts by employees and customers. I sold these businesses to a couple who were known to one of my friends. That sale was made with an installment agreement which allowed them to make payments directly to my bank to cover my loans and other outstanding debts. This agreement was made so my accounts would be taken care of while I was away from Hawaii. Unfortunately the couple did not make their payments and my obligations were not satisfied. The couple took all of my equipment from my store and disappeared. The couple spread false rumors to all my friends and the bank that I was running away without clearing my debts.

Looking for a new means to support my children, I visited my friend on Guam who I had helped when her husband was hospitalized. While there I took and passed the Guam Real Estate Test for their license. I met several Real Estate Brokers while there. I returned to Hawaii for a few days and found the negative rumors persisted. One of my Real Estate contacts in Guam asked me to return and work there. They needed licensed agents. I decided to relocate to Guam.

I called my friend on Guam. She offered to let me stay in their Guam home temporarily while I became established there. My children, then old enough to care for themselves remained in Hawaii with Lance. With $81.00 in my pocket, I flew to Guam. On arrival in Guam I remained in a hotel for one night and then, out of funds, I moved in with my friend. I went to work selling Real Estate and immediately did very well. My employer loaned me money to buy a car. Almost immediately Lance called me for money to pay his rent. I sent Lance rent money and told him to find another place to live. I told him I wanted a divorce but he would not sign for it. I moved Daniel to Guam to live with me and Cathy remained with a friend in Hawaii.

I proceeded to file for divorce which after six months became final. I was able to find Daniel a job with the contractor providing fuel for US Navy aircraft at the Guam International Airport. He soon became manager of the operation. Daniel met and married a co-worker who was from the Philippines. They now have three children. Cathy completed her studies as an Interior Decorator, married an Englishman and also has three children. I was soon able to buy a home of my own in northeast Guam near Anderson Air Force Base. It was a three bedroom, one and half bath house on a one and half acre lot.

During this time I was hired to manage the Accounting Department of a Guam based company with international assets. My major job was to prepare and file taxes for his companies which were many years behind. This company had cemeteries on the islands of Guam and Kuai, Hawaii and properties in Bremerton, Washington and Geraldton, Australia. I was told by the owner that they just needed me to help their long time accountant get their tax problems straightened out. I immediately saw it would be necessary to reorganize a very dysfunctional accounting office. I found his companies were years behind in filing taxes. Their accounting procedure for paying salesmen was out of control and there was very little knowledge of financial management throughout the staff. Their accountant had been with the company for over ten years and his procedures had never been questioned.

When I discussed a reorganization of operating procedures with the accountant, the owner and the accountant became very upset that anyone would want to change the procedures the company had been using for years. I told the owner that I would not take the job unless the accounting office deficiencies were corrected. I demanded to be paid a specific salary a month plus medical benefits and bonus at the end of the year, if all went well. I told the owner that with my system he would be able to see, within minutes, an accurate record of earnings from sales and fees due to the salesmen. Now they did not wait one to two weeks for their pay or status of their earnings to date. The old time accountant, bragging on his many years with the company, told the owner that I couldn't do what I said I could do.

I suggested to the owner that he allow me to set up a new accounting system for their facility in Kauai, Hawaii. From that action he could see my work. He agreed as I suggested and this would be my first demonstration of better organization and accounting procedures for his companies. I flew to Kauai and observed their operations for a few days and then reorganized their accounting system. I set up a new system for this office and taught them how it was to be used. I directed that they must repost all income transactions that had been received since the beginning of their operation. I remained with them for a few days until they were familiar with and could successfully operate their new system. I then returned to Guam.

In about a month the owner's daughter, who managed the Kauai cemetery, came to Guam to meet me. She introduced herself and asked if I was the Suzanne that set up the new system in Kauai. She told me that she liked the system very much. She reported to her father that her staff and salesmen liked the new accounting system and that their accounting was very accurate and timely. The owner visited the Kauai facility and liked what he saw. When he returned to Guam he fired the old accountant and I became his Accounting Manager.

The owner was a very kind and generous man with remarkable business acumen. As a young man in Hawaii he pumped gas for a living and later worked as a salesman for the largest cemetery company on Oahu. He rapidly became top sales person for that company and from that background was able to start his own cemetery on the island of Kauai. The success of that undertaking resulted in his startup of lucrative worldwide businesses. He had a son and two daughters who showed him little personal attention. He set the son up in his own business in a store selling toys, games and entertainment merchandise. This activity was not profitable due to his son spending more time playing games with his friends than attending to business.

The married daughter and the single daughter worked for their father. The father had a terminal cancer condition which he revealed to no one, not even his daughters and son. On several occasions he would become so intoxicated at his office desk that I would have to drive him home in his new Lincoln Town Car. I had observed this on the first day I met with him and his staff. There were times when he appeared so ill that, with his granddaughter, I would remain overnight at his home to be sure he would not die. The daughters were upset with me as I very often had use of his new Lincoln Town Car to conduct his personal business.

I had a difficulty with the owner's daughters who personally supported the old accountant and did not want to change from their old manual system. They eventually hired a computer expert, at great expense, to automate the entire system. After months of attempting to program everything, without my input, the system failed and they had to drop it. The owner purchased a simple computer and asked me to enter his personal business on that computer. At that time I knew very little about computers and had to do a lot of nighttime research and study to program and automate the system.

During this time, to raise funds to pay for my home, I worked three nights a week as Bartender at the club of the downtown Navy Bachelor Officers Quarters. When first asked by the club manager if I knew how to mix drinks, of course I replied yes. I immediately bought a bartenders book and became proficient behind the bar. With a good salary and tips I was able to make required payments for my house. When I would finish my bartending, usually around midnight, I would return to my accounting office and work on my computer inputs.

On my days at the office I would continue working late hours on my computer project. Some of my staff members were afraid of working late as they feared strange noises and saw unusual shadows which they perceived as harmful. When asked why I was not afraid of these perceptions I responded that these visions were real to me and that I could see and converse with them or throw them out. When asked how I could do that I did not respond. On one evening when working in the office past one in the morning I heard unusual noises. I stood up and looked around but saw nothing and returned to work. After some fifteen minutes I heard the noises again. I shouted out to whomever it might be to stand by my door. I soon had a mystical experience with clear vision of several images standing by my door. I asked for their master to appear to me. When the master appeared I asked for help with my computer setup. The response was that he didn't know computers so I chased the group away.

A friend of the owner, who was a Benedictine Monk and a computer expert, told me not to touch the computer or change any settings. He said he would set up the computer program when he returned from a two month trip to Australia. Regardless, while working late the next evening, still having problems with my computer Financial Statement set up, I prayed to God for help from the heavens. Response came immediately for me to correct my spacing and to check the punctuation in my program. On doing these things everything I had been doing cleared and I had a perfect Financial Statement appear on the screen. I had set up an automated system which worked well and was adopted by the company. On the Monk's return I told him I had already set up the system and had programmed the financial statements. The Monk was in disbelief. He asked how I had completed the programming and I told him to check the accuracy of my work. He was surprised that all was in order and advised the owner of my work. The owner was also surprised. I revealed to no one that I had the help of God.

All of my professional and personal activities were doing well but very soon I became lonely living by myself. I met many fine officers at the club but none had a very personal appeal. I prayed to God to help me solve my loneliness and God's response came clearly to me that the time will come and he will send the one for me. One evening while bartending a retired officer named Bud Smith, who was living temporarily at the Bachelor's Officers Club, stopped in for a drink. The minute he walked through the door I knew that he was the one God had sent for me.

I was impressed that he spoke a little Vietnamese having served in Vietnam during the war. He told me he had recently begun working on Guam and was looking for a house to rent or share. I told him that I had a three bedroom house and could rent a room to him. My conditions would be that he would have a bedroom, share the bathroom shower and kitchen but my bedroom would be off limits. He accepted my proposal and moved in. We lived our separate ways for the following six months, Bud was involved in establishing a Goodwill Industries operation for Guam and I in the cemetery business. We would occasionally have an evening meal together in my kitchen. Eventually our closeness developed into a mutual love and intimacy.

After Bud had been living with me for seven months I asked him to find other quarters as I had a visitor coming to visit and I needed the bedroom. When the visitor left I asked Bud to move back in with me and pay no rent. He moved back in and lived with me for another seven months. After an argument concerning my spiritual beliefs, Bud moved back to Hawaii to be with a former friend. My independent life was filled by dividing my property into four lots, selling two of the lots and building two, three bedroom homes on the others. I sold one of the homes and had enough collateral to break away from the cemetery business and start a jewelry business of my own. This was a fortunate opportunity for me to break away from the cemetery company as working with the owners daughters had made conditions for work in that office unbearable.

During this time my Mom and Nathan's family immigrated to the United States and settled in California. Almost immediately upon their arrival in the United States Nathan's wife, with their three children, left him and he was alone with Mom. He was able to get an excellent job working as a medical technician assisting disabled persons at a local hospital. The separation from his family created a mental strain on Nathan which resulted in vehicle accidents with his van and eventually a debilitating accident while riding to work on his bicycle. The injuries from that accident created physical impairment which prohibited him from work. Due to these circumstances, I brought Nathan and Mom to live with me on Guam.

Having not heard from Bud since he left Guam and not knowing where he was or what he was doing, I went to Hawaii to look for him. With guidance from above I located him and went to him. I asked him to return to Guam and to help me establish a retail and wholesale jewelry business. Bud returned to Guam with me and we immediately had the jewelry activity in business.

When I resigned from the cemetery company the owner asked me to assist, from time to time, with some of their accounting problems. A specific time came when the application for renewal of their business license was declined. I received a call from the owner to again assist in preparation of their financial statement for the Guam Business License Department which would be acceptable for license renewal. I came to the office and again found everything in disorder. The person who had taken over my position when I left was not an accountant. I immediately completed the necessary actions and the business license was granted.

As the father was becoming very ill and unable to closely manage as before, I recommended that the daughters become more involved in company operations. The younger daughter had been helping with the operation of her brother's toy store. This daughter followed my advice and became a contributing part of the overall operation. Later she came to me asking that I return to work full time. Having followed the work of the father's friend, who they thought was skilled in accounting procedures, they found he was worse than the bookkeeper. They again had some critical accounting measures that required immediate attention. I left Bud to run the jewelry business and again agreed to help them through their State audit. I corrected their accounting errors, prepared new reports and all of their business licenses were granted. The daughter agreed to let me set up an operation and accounting system for the Guam companies as I had set up in Kauai, Hawaii. I trained the younger daughter and staff on the new operations. All involved, including the salesmen, liked the new system.

I also assisted the owner's son in reconciling the books of his toy store and in the preparation of his taxes. Although frequently assisted by his sisters the son looked more often to me for advice and training in the operation of his business.

During this time the owner's personal health had deteriorated to the stage that his impact on company operations was minimal. The owner and his daughters agreed to have me set up a living trust accounting system to include all company assets. When I returned a few months later I found that the younger daughter had assumed the senior management role. A company lawyer advised the daughter to open several accounts for the different components of the company. Funds could be transferred between these accounts on a daily basis. I advised against this action as it made it easy for anyone with access to the funds to make unauthorized withdrawals.

I called attention to the work of a clerk, who the daughter trusted, of a missing check for $6,000.00. I recommend that clerk be terminated before more funds turned up missing. The daughter said that clerk was doing a good job and she would not fire her. After a few months they again found funds missing and that the thief was that clerk. The daughter now realized that what I had previously related about the clerk was true and the clerk was fired.

In 1992, Bud and I went to Vietnam to determine if there were business opportunities there. This was a few years before the United States resumed ties with Vietnam. We quickly found that Communist domination continued to be very strict and that it was not advisable to pursue business in Vietnam at that time.

One Monday morning, after a long weekend, Bud returned to the jewelry store and found display counters broken and all of the gold jewelry and precious stones had been stolen. Thieves had broken through the wall of an adjacent office for entry. Fortunately I had taken the high valued diamonds home with me for that weekend. Insurance did not cover this very extensive loss. This was the end of a successful jewelry operation in Guam.

As the administrative work for the company began to pile up on me, I recommended to the owner that Bud be hired to assist me with the administrative work and to help the second daughter monitor the construction of a mortuary and chapel being built at the site of the Guam Memorial Park Cemetery. I helped Bud learn the paperwork involved in running the cemetery business and the required administrative work.

Bud listened but would not take direction from anyone, including me. On one occasion he even shouted me down in front of others which I felt demeaning to me. This was the beginning of my having a more difficult time working with the daughters and the staff. Little annoyances such as argument over my use of a parking spot, authorized to me by the father, and that a daughter wanted for salesmen. Also I began to get a hard time from the bookkeeper who was afraid I would let her go due to subpar work caused by her following the previous accounting manager's erroneous guidance.

As the owner became more ill he had a more difficult time understanding our telephonic conversations. The daughters hired a previous consultant, Herman, who spoke better English than I. He was well grounded in computer operations but did not know much about cemetery operations and management. They had him work with the bookkeeper on inputting accounting information and filing tax data. The taxes had not been filed since I left the company. The company paid him $50.00 an hour for over two years.

When I checked his work I found many errors. I went to the daughters and explained the difficulties. I explained that they had paid $50.00 an hour for a lot of incorrect data entered into the computer system. I told them that I did not think Herman knew enough about the business to do the work required. I suggested that they let him go. Regardless, Herman was able to convince them that his actions were correct and they retained his services. The daughters suggested that I go before Herman. In just a few months the daughter began having problems with the Government of Guam for failure to file back taxes. The second daughter realized that they should have listened to me and let Herman go. She wanted to sue Herman for his failures but he was long gone and they found they could do nothing but correct the errors.

Before the father died he confided in me that he was concerned about the overall status of the company. I told him I would do my best to take care of it. After a few weeks the working conditions became uncomfortable and I decided to go into a new business for myself. I was able to get the cemetery office working smoothly and told the daughters I was leaving but would be available if they needed help in the future.

I learned that there were business opportunities on the neighboring island of Saipan. I sold my house and moved with Mom and Nathan to Saipan. Bud remained with the cemetery company. On Saipan I was able to lease a building near the beach and on a main thoroughfare which provided display cases for jewelry, office space for my Certified Public Accounting, Real Estate businesses and living quarters. I immediately opened a jewelry store and business office. We were close enough to the ocean that Mom was able to have frequent, comfortable walks on the beach.

I quickly learned that Saipan, as a United States Territory, allowed sponsored H-2 immigrants to open businesses and to do any job available. I hired several H-2 workers to assist in accounting and tax preparation. I sponsored them in order that they remain on Saipan. Most of the immigrants were from the Philippines and accepted very low wages. I experienced limited income from my businesses as most of my customers could not afford my fees and frequently defaulted on payments for services and or purchases. The only jewelry items that they would purchase from me were those of the lowest value. The buyers, who had money, would fly to Guam to shop where there were larger department stores and more selections and competitive priced items available. After a short time on the Island my brother Nathan met and married a Philippine lady who had one son. I arranged a very elaborate wedding ceremony which was performed by the Governor of Saipan at his official residence on the island.

After a year of disappointing business I decided to return to the mainland of the United States. I flew to New Jersey with Mom and stayed with a friend until I could get settled. My daughter, Cathy, convinced me to come to North Carolina where she lived with her family. Mom and I moved to Charlotte, North Carolina and found a comfortable apartment there.

I was able to find temporary work for a Certified Public Accountant in Charlotte. I worked at night in the accounting office of the Hanniford grocery store chain. My work at the grocery was to lead to a full time job as an Assistant Manager. I had to quickly learn the functions of the different departments such as produce, butchering, frozen foods and of cashiering. I also had to learn the handling of funds which included selling money orders, Western Union operations, setting key approval codes, counting, balancing and approving cashier transactions and familiarization with all financial transactions.

On the first day in the position as bookkeeper I was trained by an instructor from a different branch of the grocery store chain. On my second day I had a telephone call from a bookkeeper from another Hanniford store branch asking me for help in balancing her work. I couldn't respond immediately but learned from my computer that night and gave her the answers the next morning. I was surprised to hear that my managing bookkeeper could not believe that I had solved the problems of the other branch store. They had this problem before and couldn't believe that I had solved their long standing problem. I found that there were many other similar accounting difficulties.

After working for four days as bookkeeper, an instructor from another branch of Hanniford stores came to provide me additional instruction. His actions were questionable as he spent more time talking on the phone with friends than helping me. He had me count one departing cashier's change box and everything balanced. While he was there he had me take a break. At the end of the day I balanced all work of the day. Significantly when I recounted the funds in the cashier's box that the instructor had done with me it was short ten dollars. The loss was obvious.

My heavy workload each night was to finalize and balance all accounts before midnight. I was frequently interrupted after nine PM by counter work selling cigarettes, video rentals, money orders and Western Union entries. There was a large sign posted that there were to be no such actions after nine PM. One evening, after eleven PM, a lady came to send a Western Union money order. I refused her request and she became furious and reported me to the manager. The next night the manager condemned me for not helping the customer. I responded that I did not have the time to help the customer and to complete my accounting requirements. I reminded the manager that we had a clearly displayed sign that there would be no such actions after nine PM. I was surprised when the manager told me that this was just a sign and not company policy. I walked away in frustration.

After working as a cashier for over two months, with no sign of promotion, I went to the manager and questioned why I had not been assigned to the position of bookkeeper and assistant manager for which I had applied. She said I would have to wait. When I helped at a different branch they had liked my work and I had no problem learning the super market business. Not wanting to wait, I went to the manager of the branch store and asked to be transferred to their store. I was told that I would have to have a transfer approved by the losing branch. When I returned to my basic branch my manager asked me why I wanted to change locations. I told her that I had waited too long for the job and wages that I had been promised. The next day she gave me a raise and I was made Assistant Manager of the store. This became a very successful adventure as the job went well and I received the praises of all with whom I worked, below and above my status.

Bud decided to leave Guam and be with me in the United States. He was hired by Holiday Retirement Corporation, a company from Salem, Oregon which owned and operated exclusive Senior Independent Living Retirement complexes across the United States. The position required couples to serve as managers, to live in their facilities and to manage all functions from rentals, maintenance, housekeeping, foodservice and transportation. Concurrently, the managers were to plan, organize and direct senior activities for residents of the facility. I decided to go with Bud. I gave the Hanniford Company two week notice that I would resign. My manager pleaded with me to stay as she considered me an asset to her operations. She even offered me a raise in pay. The company gave me a nice farewell party before I departed.

Bud and I joined another couple as Assistant Managers of a Holiday Retirement Corporation facility in Durham, North Carolina, "Durham Regent". After a few weeks we joined another couple to gain a different experience in a new Durham facility, "Emerald Pond". Each of these retirement homes provided comfortable private apartments for over 250 healthy, independent living, senior citizens. For additional training we joined another managing couple at a third facility in Wilmington, North Carolina, "Lake Shore Commons".

After a few months we were transferred to Gainesville, Georgia as Managers of our own facility,

"Smoky Springs". Bud and I gave the residents very personal care and attention to keep their spirits high and enjoy their aging lifestyle. Using my nursing skills I assisted them when they were ill and aided their physical conditioning with exercise routines such as Tai Chi and Yoga. At each of our locations we became very attached to the residents and they became very close to us. On one occasion the residents sent a petition to the Holiday Retirement Corporation headquarters asking that we not be transferred. It was difficult for us to leave each group of seniors with whom we had become personally attached.

While in Georgia, we moved Mom and Nathan to a comfortable apartment not far from our facility. During that time Bud received word from his daughter that their mother had died of a heart attack. He returned to Colorado Springs, Colorado to settle her estate. He deeded the property to his son and drove an old Buick back to Georgia retaining a few selections from a family art collection.

Holiday Retirement Corporation, constructing a new facility in Ocala, Florida, offered Bud and me the management position for that activity. We accepted that challenge and moved to Ocala with Mom and Nathan. We found a two bedroom apartment next door to our new independent living complex. We arrived to find that construction of the new building had been delayed and the move in date for the new residents had to be changed. Unfortunately, our Holiday sales staff had already sold 25 apartments for immediate occupancy. We had to arrange with the local Hilton Hotel to house these projected tenants. We had to provide rooms and meals for these 25 seniors for the next twenty-three days. The Hilton took very good care of us, providing every need and courtesies for our tenants.

Soon after we moved in to the new facility and began to get everything organized and running smooth the Regional Manager for Holiday directed Bud to return to the facility "Smoky Springs" in Georgia to help the management there. They had experienced a drop in "move ins" since we departed. While Bud was gone I had to run our new facility and handle all requirements myself. I had a couple for Assistant Managers but they were slow to learn the job. They were lazy and non-productive and rarely followed my guidance and instruction. I was working until midnight most nights to get all management activities completed. I learned that they were sending negative reports on me to the Region Manager to avoid work I directed for them. The Region Manager's wife came in to assist me during Bud's absence.

When Bud returned from Georgia he learned he had a mild cancer affliction and suggested that we retire. I was ready to leave the Holiday Retirement Corporation but did not want to completely retire. I wanted to remain in the accounting or real estate business. I felt I still had the responsibility for caring for my Mom and my brother Nathan. I did not want Bud to have to take care of them.

We retired and bought a comfortable home on a one acre lot in a nice residential area of Ocala. The home was one story, ranch style, with a large yard, easy for Mom and Nathan to move around. Mom continued to live an active life to her 105th year. She took part in meal preparation and always had coffee ready in the morning. Following a simple accident, getting out of bed one morning, her activities rapidly declined. Her condition deteriorated to the point that she could not stand or sit down without assistance. Although I was much lighter than Mom, I had to pick her up and lay her down many times a day. After several times hospitalized, she passed away June 24, 2009, at the age of 105.

As we settled into a new life style I was able to involve myself in more community activities. I was invited to become a member of The Ocala Royal Dames for Cancer Research, a volunteer organization dedicated to raising funds for cancer research. This group of ladies raised funds primarily in support of the Shands Cancer Research Center at the University of Florida, the Moffitt Cancer Center in Tampa and the College of Central Florida Nursing program here in Ocala. I soon became a member of the Ocala Royal Dames' Board of members. One of my initial actions was to advise the Chairman of the Funding Allocations Committee on problems with their records and reports. I recommended that before any more funds were provided the activity receiving the funds must report what they had done with the funds we provided in the past. Also they would be required to provide their plans for use of future funding. My recommendations were accepted.

I was appointed to be chairperson for In-Kind Donations. I found that, since the beginning, there had never been a specific format for donors or purchasers for these donations. I developed and printed such formats which are in use today. During that time I was chairman and director of a special event, a Hawaiian Luau, which resulted in raising over $14,000.00 for cancer research. The Ocala Royal Dames for Cancer Research has raised over $3,000,000.00 since the organization became chartered.

I was also a board member and Vice President of the Ladies Auxiliary of the Military Officers Association of America involved in community activities. One year, working with the Ocala "Stuff-the-Bus Program", I organized and ran a Hawaiian Luau, similar to the activity the year before, which collected over $17,000.00 for support of some 1,200 homeless children in Marion County Florida Public Schools.

During these times, a friend had agreed to sponsor a Vietnamese lady and her daughter emigrating from a refugee camp in the Philippines. The friend found that she could not support this family and asked if I could help. I agreed and I took the lady and daughter into my home. I provided them a room, bath and a separate kitchen to prepare their own meals. After a week I found them regular work in a local hospital. They continued to work, live comfortably and quickly assimilate into their new American way of life. In several months they felt they should go out on their own and not be a burden to me. They moved to a larger city and found work, successfully demonstrating their positive work ethic and talent. Within a year they opened their own business and now have a home of their own.

Since I have been in the United States I have had the opportunity to assist many Vietnamese as they immigrated and became established in their new environ. I have been able to assist many in translating documents, interpreting verbal transactions and even providing transportation when required. There were times, even when I was not flush with funds, that I loaned money to those in need.

In August of 2009, Bud and I had the opportunity to visit with family and friends. In August we to drove to Murfreesboro, Tennessee for the birthday celebration of my daughter Cathy and my son Daniel. In May of the following year we again drove to Murfreesboro for the High School graduation of granddaughters, Samantha and Ericka. We drove from that event on to attend the graduation of Bud's granddaughter, Kim Cowan, from the U.S. Military Academy at West Point, New York. In June of 2010, Cathy, Daniel and I flew to Kansas City, Missouri for the wedding of Raymond Kirtland's daughter. All were exciting events.

In my free time I completed the final proof of my International Cookbook, with recipes from 16 different countries, for the printers. On December 10, 2010, I received 38 boxes of beautifully printed, hard back covered cook books. In addition to sales, the books made very appropriate Christmas gifts for relatives and friends.

Nathan passed away, January 14, 2012

Nathan's physical condition deteriorated rapidly. Treatment by the doctors at the University of Florida, Shands Neurological Center, determined that Nathan was suffering from a very rare, inherited disease of the brain called "Machado-Joseph Disease" which progressively causes degeneration of muscle control and coordination of the upper and lower extremities. Nathan also experienced difficulty with speech and swallowing. First identified, worldwide, in 1985, there is no known cure for this disease. Nathan was treated for over three years by the doctors at the University of Florida, Shands Neurological Center with little or no change in his continued physical deterioration.

On February 15, 2011, I flew with Nathan to Vietnam to see if there was anything in that area of the world which could be done to cure his disease. After three months I flew home leaving Nathan in the care of our sister Cuc. After seven months with no positive results for a cure for Nathan's illness there, I flew to Ho Chi Minh City and brought Nathan home on September 15, 2011. As with Mom, many times a day I had to lift Nathan and assist him physically in any way necessary. After several hospitalizations, Nathan died January 14, 2012. At the Hospital's request his remains were provided to Shands Neurological Center for autopsy and further research on the rare "Machado-Joseph Disease". The costs for both Mom's and Nathan's hospitalization were overwhelming.

While Nathan was still alive, on May 16, 2011, my son Daniel arrived from Tennessee, having divorced his family and looking for a new start in life. Since I needed funds to pay hospital debts and Daniel needed work, I organized a commercial cleaning business to provide post construction cleaning for local contractors. We worked first with another established cleaning firm but soon branched out and solicited our own private contracts. That enterprise continues with regular work but has not been as successful as I had anticipated. One contractor, citing unsubstantiated errors in our work, failed to pay several thousand dollars for work properly completed. The last contractor was so pleased with our work that they asked for our participation in their future projects. In pursuit of a new business venture I am now in a joint partnership established to open and manage a Vietnamese specialty restaurant in Ocala. I will be financing this activity with the assistance of friends and relatives. We hope our restaurant will open for business sometime in the year, 2018.

I am now living an active and enjoyable life with Bud in our comfortable home, running my businesses, involved in community affairs and assisting those in need when the circumstance arises.

These words describing the wonders of my life are true as written. The varied experiences of my Mom and me, while on this earth relate many challenges and serious difficulties which were overcome. Although many times I failed to respond effectively to the experiences I faced, my actions were taken for the best interest of those around me. I depended on the guidance of God to lead me in the right direction. I truly feel that by continuing to believe in the teachings of God and following his orders there is a spiritual purpose for me in this world. In time true peace and happiness will be achieved.

Suzanne Smith

ABOUT THE BIOGRAPHER

Suzanne Smith is a dynamic entrepreneur, who from very humble beginnings, during the ravages of the Vietnam War, through years of personal hardships, obtaining a BA Degree, and devotion to the wellbeing of her children, has become a leader in her community and a positive influence to all with whom she is associated. In the time of war, she participated with the American forces in their interactions with the Vietnamese culture. As the Communist took over the country she was a dominate force in the actions needed to evacuate the last of the Vietnamese-American orphans from the country. After settling in the United States she quickly assimilated to her new surroundings and immediately became a self-sufficient, contributing member of her community. She now owns and operates her own company and is an active participant with organizations raising funds in support of community projects. She gives credit for her successes through life to her close association with God.

CPSIA information can be obtained
at www.ICGtesting.com
Printed in the USA
FFHW010726250419
51993512-57404FF